OTHER BOOKS BY THE AUTHOR

Talk to God and Fix Your Health:
The Real Reasons Why We Get Sick and How to Stay Healthy

49 Days:
An Interactive Journal of Self-Development

The Happy Workshop:
An Eight Week Journey to Real, Lasting Happiness

PEOPLE SMARTS: THE SYSTEM

UNDERSTAND OTHERS, UNDERSTAND YOURSELF AND CRUSH YOUR STRESS

RIVKA LEVY

The mind is man's very essence.

- Rebbe Nachman of Breslov

CONTENTS

INTRODUCTION

Thousands of years ago, the greatest Greek philosophers understood that the human personality is made up of four primary states. In the ancient world, these were linked to the four 'elements' that they believed the whole world, including human beings, consisted of.

The four elements of the ancient world were termed: FIRE, AIR, WATER and EARTH, and the ancients believed that getting these four elements in 'balance' was the key to happiness, health and good emotional health. (It goes without saying that being happy and emotionally-healthy enables people to develop and maintain loving, healthy and durable relationships with other people.)

But then, beginning in the Victorian era, modern science took over the reins of dealing with the human psyche, and the 'four elements' approach of the ancient world was forgotten. Western medicine veered strongly away from the 'holistic', whole-person approach to dealing with people and their problems, and concentrated instead on breaking everything down into its smallest parts.

Over the last 20 years, something of a consensus approach has started to emerge between those who view people and their minds as nothing more than a collection of chemical reactions, and those who are stuck in an old-world philosophy that apparently bears no relationship to the findings of modern science.

To describe it in its most basic terms, what the scientists started to discover is that the main reason that people can behave in unhelpful, socially-unacceptable and even pathological ways is because they've experienced a lot of stress and trauma in their lives.

Our brains can react in some very dramatic ways to stress. You've probably already heard about the FIGHT-FLIGHT response to stress, where we either try to fight out way out of a tight corner, or run away from a danger or threat, but there are actually two additional common stress states. Science is still trying to figure out exactly what to call them, but for the purposes of this book, I'm officially naming them the "FREEZE" and "FLATTER" stress responses.

I spent five long years learning everything about FIGHT, FLIGHT, FREEZE and FLATTER, or what I'll call the '4Fs', for short, when one day I realized an amazing thing: modern science and the ancients sages were simply using different words to talk about exactly the same thing.

Science's 4Fs were actually just a modern description of the ancient world's four elements.

The FIRE of the ancient Greeks was clearly talking about the FIGHT stress response, where our temper can flare up, and an angry outburst can scorch anyone unfortunate enough to be within striking distance.

AIR describes the FLIGHT response, that tendency to run away at the first hint of trouble and disappear into thin air, literally and figuratively.

As the only element that can freeze into ice, the ancient Greeks' WATER element obviously referred to the FREEZE stress state, where we disappear into our own bubbles and go into hibernation to avoid having to deal with an overwhelming and disappointing world.

And so, that left the dependable, solid and stoic EARTH element, which correlate to modern science's FLATTER stress response, where we let people tread all over us and exploit us for their own ends.

As you might have noticed, science tends to focus on all the *negative* aspects of the human personality, and on all the yucky and crazy stuff people can do when they get overwhelmed by stress. But the ancient world, with their broader, and dare I say *healthier* view of people, created a framework that focused far more on what a balanced human personality could look like.

The ancient sages were telling us that if you got all your elements working together and stayed focused on balancing out reactions to stress, there would be no stopping you! This book will show you how to do that.

In the following pages you'll learn about the 16 different PEOPLE SMARTS personality types; you'll discover how stress can make you act and over-react in specific ways that often put tremendous strain on your relationships and ability to function; and most importantly, you'll learn to understand yourself – and other people – so much better, so you start to play to your strengths, minimize your weaknesses, and most importantly, **start to really like yourself.**

Or, to put this another way:

If you're sick of over-reacting to things that are really no big deal, blowing up at people you love, melting down into overwhelm when even the smallest thing goes wrong, running away instead of facing up to a mistake, or switching off whenever your nearest and dearest is trying to tell you something very important – I have good news for you.

That can all change.

The People Smarts System will explain how so many of your unhelpful habits and destructive reactions came about. It will help you to identify why you are responding the way you are, underline key negative behaviors to start working on, and then set out core habits you can develop that will help you regain balance and tap into the awesome power of your particular personality type.

The focus of this book is on moving from 'unbalanced and unhappy' to 'balanced and fulfilled', and not on dwelling on how you got 'unbalanced' in the first place.

In the following pages, we'll take a look at the four main stress responses and how these '4Fs' are responsible for pretty much every unhelpful and destructive emotional issue you're experiencing in life.

Then, we'll learn about the full PEOPLE SMARTS 16 personality system, which will help you figure out how your own personal reaction to stress may be tripping you up and holding you back in life. But we won't stop there, because we're also going to describe the tremendous potential that each one of the 16 personality types contain when they're balanced, and set out a blueprint for how you can start to live life to the full – as yourself! - and enjoy meaningful, loving and healthy relationships.

Once you start to understand what makes you and the people in your life really tick, you will find it so much easier to defuse relationship issues before they even begin, simply by understanding why everyone is reacting the way they are.

While the ideas I'm going to share with you are very powerful, this is not a book of magic or 'quick fixes'.

Your reactions and over-reactions to stress were learned over many years, and it's going to take some time and effort before your brain starts consistently acting and reacting the way you'd like it to. This is a life-long learning process, and there will always be room for improvement.

But what I can promise you is that even if all you do is read this book from start to finish, by the time you reach the last page, I guarantee you will understand yourself, and what's really making you -- and others -- tick, way more than you would even after many years of standard therapy. And that understanding, all by itself, will kick-start the process of helping you regain your emotional balance in some fundamental and far-reaching ways, even if you choose to do nothing else with the information.

But if you want to take things further, the sky is really the limit. If you'd like to learn more about how to apply the PEOPLE SMARTS SYSTEM to different areas of your life and your relationships, the RESOURCES section at the back can point you in the direction of some other ways you can do that.

Don't be fooled by the apparent simplicity of what you're about to learn. The PEOPLE SMARTS SYSTEM isn't guesswork, it's scientifically proven, and can teach us how to move to a place of greater balance, inner peace and harmony with the people around us.

I wanted to keep this book easy to read and easy to apply, so I deliberately kept it short and 'unscientific'. But if anyone who is interested in exploring the more scientific side of things, you'll find a list of interesting books and other resources at the back of this book, that can guide you towards

Before we dive in, let me tell you how the *People Smarts* system came into being. For years and years, I was struggling with a lot of overwhelming reactions to stress that were making me miserable, taking me out of action, and causing me a lot of issues with the people around me.

As a **Philosopher-Motivator** personality type, I fell into severe depressions that could leave me crying in bed for days and even weeks at a time. Or I could flip into feelings of incandescent rage at the smallest challenge or disappointment.

For years I just tried to keep things together and manage, but like many people who over-react to stress, I found I was developing something of a Dr. Jekyll and Mr. Hyde personality where I never knew when the reaction to stress would take over and leave me feeling either depressed and despairing, or raging like an angry maniac with an almost irresistible urge to drop everything and run away.

When I wasn't reacting to stress, I was kind, calm, collected, and generally nice to be around. But when that switch got flipped… watch out!

It was really only when my first daughter was born that I realized I had to stop pretending everything was fine and come to grips with what was really going on. At that stage, I started spending hundreds of dollars a week talking about my difficult childhood with a large collection of therapists.

It was useful in terms of validating my experiences, but in terms of making my depressions a thing of the past, or taking down my temper, if anything, the therapy often just made things worse. I hit a dead-end where the only option on the table seemed to be medication. Thankfully, my inner 'Motivator' kicked in at that point and I realized two things:

1) There had to be an answer to dealing with my emotional problems that didn't involve pills 2) I wasn't going to find that answer within the framework of conventional therapy

From that point on, my inner 'Philosopher' came to the fore and I started researching everything I could find about dealing with stress across a range of disciplines, including:

- Energy Psychology
- Chinese Medicine
- Somatic (body-based) therapies
- Trauma, PTSD and Complex-PTSD research
- Nutrition, especially the impact of vitamin and mineral deficiency on brain-functioning
- Mindfulness and daily meditation

At the end of that research process I discovered that so-called 'broken brains' could be fixed, that traumatic experiences can shape our personalities and reactions, particularly under stress – and that even the most unhelpful over-reactions to stress can be tamed, ameliorated and balanced-out over time, *once we understand what's really causing them.*

That information literally changed my life.

Once I knew my depressive states were an extreme reaction to stress, I could pinpoint exactly what type of 'stress' was subconsciously sparking them off, and then stop them in their tracks. At the time of writing, I haven't been depressed in three years.

While I still sometimes get angry, I lose control way, way less frequently, and I'm getting more adept all the time at spotting the warning signs that my stress is approaching 'overwhelming' levels, so I can take the action required to defuse it before I say or do something I might really regret.

As a result, so many of my relationships are blossoming in a way that was simply unthinkable beforehand, and I've gone from feeling strung out, anxious and moody to feeling calm, confident and content most of the time.

Now, I want to share what I learned with you.

Anyone can learn the *People Smarts* system, and everyone can apply it in a way that will help them to literally transform the way they relate to themselves, to others, and to how they respond to the challenges and issues we all experience in life.

So without any further ado, let's take the first step of this journey and learn more about the four main building blocks of the human personality.

THE FOUR BUILDING BLOCKS OF PERSONALITY

For many millennia, human beings have been trying to understand how the world around them really works and operates. The ancient Chinese came up with the 'Five Elements' theory to try to explain the interactions they saw within the physical world, and also to codify some of the penetrating insights they had developed into human health and the human psyche.

Even today, the Five Elements theory underpins the practice of Chinese Medicine and the ancient Chinese understanding of the subtle, bio-electric dimension of the human body. This is something modern science is still scrambling to catch up with in our times.

By contrast, the ancient Greeks and ancient Hebrews developed a theory based on just four elements, that of FIRE, AIR, WATER and EARTH, to try to describe the physical world. Over time, further tweaks were made to this basic recipe, most notably by Aristotle, the famous Greek philosopher who lived in the 4th century BCE. The Four Elements theory was a foundation of scientific thought for more than 2,000 years.

The theory appeared to be logical, as so much of the natural world seemed to be easily divided up into 'fours'. There are four seasons, four winds, and back then, the body was considered to have four main organs, namely the liver, lungs, heart and kidneys. The ancient peoples also believed that Man was created from a combination of these four elements, FIRE, AIR, WATER and EARTH, and this view held sway in the early medical profession until the late medieval times, with a number of highly-respected treatises being written about the 'four humors' that were said to govern human health.

But towards the end of the 18th century modern science began to come into its own, and the four elements as a scientific theory of how the physical world operates was consigned to history books. The final nail in its coffin occurred in 1869, when the first periodic table of elements was composed by Dmitri Mendeleev, which divided the physical world into more than 100 elements, and not just the four elements of the ancient Greeks.

From that point on, the four elements became the preserve of mystics and astrologers instead of the mainstay of the physical sciences.

Ancient people approached the world in a much more holistic way than modern man. Instead of the modern preoccupation of dividing everything up into smaller and smaller areas of expertise and specialization, the ancients tended to view things as a much bigger picture. They wanted to understand how the world, and the people in it, worked as a complete system.

This 'holistic' approach was also reflected in the poetic way they described many of their observations and insights. The four elements was not so much a literal description of how the physical world operates, as it was a metaphorical description of how the physical *forces* in the world and the psychological phenomena within the human mind operate in tangent with each other.

The ancients weren't so much describing the human body with the four elements as they were the human psyche, or personality.

When I started researching how the human personality works and is developed I started reading a great deal about what modern science called the 'stress response'. We'll get into that topic in way more detail further on in the book, but one day I had a Eureka! moment that the four main stress responses being described by modern psychology were a direct reflection of the four elements of the human psyche described in the ancient world.

FIRE mapped to the **FIGHT** response.

AIR mapped to the **FLIGHT** response.

WATER mapped to the **FREEZE** response.

EARTH mapped to the **FLATTER** response.

This was one of the most satisfying connections I think I've ever made in the almost 10 years I've been studying the human personality. Over the next two years I started to fill out what these four basic 'building blocks' of the human personality actually consisted of, and to identify the underlying quality, or energy, that each was imparting to the human personality.

IDENTIFYING THE FOUR BUILDING BLOCKS

By contrasting and comparing the ancient world's descriptions of the characteristics associated with the four elements of FIRE, AIR, WATER and EARTH with modern science's descriptions of how the four stress responses of FIGHT, FLIGHT, FREEZE and FLATTER could shape the human personality, I managed to build up a comprehensive list of the main positive and negative characteristics of each of the four main building blocks of personality.

The next step was to find a better way of describing these four building blocks. I toyed with reverting back to the ancient world's description of the four elements, but I realized that with their modern association with astrology and the occult, they just weren't going to work for the PEOPLE SMARTS SYSTEM.

At the same time, I didn't want to get stuck simply describing each building block via their stress response, as that was painting a very negative and one-dimensional picture of the tremendous positive potential each of these modes actually contains.

So I kept revisiting the list of character traits for FIRE / FIGHT, AIR / FLIGHT, WATER / FREEZE, and EARTH / FLATTER, searching for a suitable modern description that I could use for the PEOPLE SMARTS SYSTEM that would fully capture the energy contained in each personality building block.

After a lot of trial and error, I came up with the following descriptor which captures the basic essence and energy of the four building blocks:

FIRE / FIGHT = MOTIVATION

AIR / FLIGHT = COMMUNICATION

WATER / FREEZE = PHILOSOPHICAL THINKING

EARTH / FLATTER = BUILDING

All of us contain these four building blocks in our personalities in greater or lesser amounts. Even those of us who are predominantly reacting from a place of MOTIVATION, for example, will sometimes also approach life from a point of PHILOSOPHICAL THINKING, or a BUILDING place. The more balanced our personality becomes, the more we will be able to access modes of thinking, behaving and reacting that are contained in one of our non-dominant building blocks.

When balanced, a passionate MOTIVATOR personality can learn how to sometimes defer to others while, over time, a more passive BUILDER personality can learn how to balance out their tendency to please others with the important skill of looking after their own interests, too.

Each of the four building blocks of personality contains tremendous power and potential – and also some notable dangers and pitfalls.

Over the rest of this chapter, I'm going to properly introduce you to these four building blocks so you can begin the process of understanding how the human psyche really works.

HOW TO USE THIS INFORMATION

As you read through these descriptions, try to see which 'building block' speaks to you the most. Which seems to capture more of your essence, and more of your character traits? It can also be useful to consider which building blocks seem to most describe close family members, friends, or maybe even your boss at work.

The more we understand how the human personality is essentially made up of different admixtures of the following four building blocks, the easier it will be to understand how and why we act and react the way we do, particularly under stress, and also how we interact with the people around us.

A little later on, we'll break these four main building blocks into detailed descriptions of the 16 main PEOPLE SMARTS SYSTEM personalities, which will give us a wealth of clues and insights into how we operate in the world, and what our main motivations and fears are.

In the following chapter, you can also take the PEOPLE SMARTS SYSTEM quiz, which has been designed to make it as easy as possible for you figure out which personality type you might be. But before you take the quiz, take some time to learn about each of the building blocks in turn, because as I stated above, all of us are a mix of all four of them.

While identifying our PEOPLE SMARTS SYSTEM personality type will help us to understand what our starting point might be for our personalities, and particularly, how our personalities might react under stress, the goal of the PEOPLE SMARTS SYSTEM is to move us towards achieving more balance.

And that means identifying some of the traits or characteristics contained in our non-dominant personality building blocks that we'd like to attain, and then over time, working on acquiring them. Again, all of us contain all four of the building blocks described below, it's just that they are more obvious in some people, and more latent in others. But they are there, and like a muscle, they can be built up and developed over time.

The other thing I want to stress before we begin this journey is that everything can change! Our personality types are not fixed in stone. As we become less reactive to stress and less prone to polarizing to a particular stress response, we enable our minds to start developing the more positive characteristics and traits associated with our particular PEOPLE SMARTS SYSTEM personality typology.

And that's when the magic really begins!

So without any more ado, let's dive in and take a look at the first building block.

BUILDING BLOCK 1: MOTIVATION

There's a famous proverb that even the longest journey begins with the first step – and MOTIVATION is what gets a person to take that step, and to start moving. MOTIVATION gets us out of bed in the morning; it keeps us studying for our exams late at night; it can help us to continue going when everyone else has given up, and it contains the rawest energy of all of the four building blocks.

MOTIVATION is all about the power of transformation, and when we have a big helping of MOTIVATION in our personalities, we will be a force to be reckoned with in the world.

Motivators can light up a room – or burn it down. When this characteristic is expressed in a positive and controlled way, Motivators can be extremely inspiring, passionate and vibrant. You'll often find them in the center of all the action, and their enthusiasm and energy for their pet projects can be extremely contagious.

Motivators can spark off discussions, brainstorming sessions – and revolutions – like no-one else. They often move fast, and will be described by others as a bundle of energy. They can be generous big spenders, mesmerizing entertainers, and often dramatic and flamboyant.

Motivators are go-getters, and make a powerful impact on their surroundings. With their colorful self-expression and fearlessness, they can instantly transform boring to exciting, bland to piquant, and quiet to boisterous. When properly applied and channeled, the energy of Motivation makes things happen, and fast. Motivation can spread quickly, and it doesn't wait for others to keep up with it.

Motivators are intense in the moment, but they require a lot of raw material – like attention, praise and support - to keep burning with such passion and enthusiasm long-term.

A very strong Motivator can be unstoppable. They can wrap other people around their little fingers and bulldoze their way through any obstacle or fence that might be stopping them from getting where they want to go. This is a very useful ability – but it has to be used responsibly and judiciously, because when all that motivation is applied in the wrong place, or to the wrong goals, it can have terrible and often unintended consequences.

When Motivation is misplaced, wrong or negative, things can quickly get out of control. Motivators are rarely timid and retiring, so when things start to go wrong, everyone knows about it.

Depending on how volatile the Motivation is, a small spark is often all that's required to set off an enormous explosion. At the same time, a little Motivation can often be a very fragile thing, and easily extinguished, so Motivation sometimes has to be nurtured carefully, and coaxed along.

In its unbalanced state, Motivation is often powered by the energy of self-interest, or 'me first'. Strong motivators typically don't like sharing the limelight or rewards with others, often racing towards their goals to try to get there first. They can be highly competitive, and can also become greedy, as the Motivation becomes overly fixated on securing personal gain and advantage, even at other people's expense.

Motivation often takes no prisoners, and when thwarted or blocked in some way, it can degenerate into negative traits including anger, rage, hatred and harsh criticism.

Motivators often have a pronounced spiritual or mystical side, and can be deeply intuitive, but they don't come by their insight in a linear fashion. The type of understanding associated with Motivation often occurs as more of a lightning strike, or Eureka! moment that can't be taught, or sometimes even really expressed to other people. It's a sense of knowing something, a form of internal 'prophecy' that has to be taken on its own merits, and can't really be explained.

While Motivation's intuition can often be keenly accurate, it can also be totally off-base, which can sometimes lead the Motivator to imagine slights that have never occurred, and to create vendettas and arguments over things that never really happened.

With all their passion, insight and strength of character, Motivators are often very courageous and brave, and will go to bat to defend causes they believe in, even at a very high personal cost. Motivators aren't scared to act, and can often inspire others with their determination and fortitude, even in the face of enormous challenges.

Their mix of charisma, courage and passion can make Motivators natural leaders. They tend to gravitate into a central place within organizational structures, families and communities. Motivators naturally command a lot of attention, and two of the other personality types, Communicators and Builders, are naturally drawn towards them.

The personality types who usually have the strongest antipathy for Motivators are the Philosophers and perhaps ironically, other Motivators. Typically, gurus, visionaries and divas find it hard to get along with each other, particularly if they're trying to motivate their colleagues towards conflicting goals or aims.

Often, when you're dealing with an unbalanced Motivator, the only people who can get them to behave in a fairer or more reasonable way to others will be another strong Motivator. Most of the other personality types will lack the sticking power, courage or strength to actually take them on and successfully confront them.

A balanced Motivator can put out an awful lot of illumination, inspiration and clarity into the world, and can use their passion and ability to interest and excite others and make them feel truly loved, seen, and a part of something much greater than themselves. Motivators make uplifting leaders, popular teachers, and firebrand preachers of whatever creed or belief has caught their imagination.

An unbalanced Motivator can also draw big crowds, but may do this by being deliberately controversial and provocative, arrogantly puffing themselves up while destroying the reputations and prospects of others they view as 'competition'. Strong Motivators take no prisoners, and will shoot to kill in their arguments and disagreements, so unless you're someone who has the stomach for a fight, the best course of action is usually to just steer clear of an unbalanced or unreasonably aggressive Motivator.

Motivators can keep arguments and vendettas passionately raging for years, and with incredible intensity, long after everyone else would have given up and gone home. When this tendency is balanced, it turns into a tremendous willpower and a strong determination to see things through to the end, no matter what obstacles or challenges are in the way.

Most, if not all, all of the social, political, religious or economic revolutions that have occurred in the world had a strong Motivator at their helm. No other personality type has the guts to light the first match, or the sheer bull-headed commitment to see the thing through, no matter what.

As a rule, Motivators are the most assertive of all the elements, and in the unbalanced state they can find it very difficult to respect boundaries, and to follow rules, especially in the heat of the moment. When the heat is on, Motivators usually polarize to the FIGHT Stress Response, and will come out swinging.

While their negative behavior can often degenerate into bullying, throwing tantrums and threatening others to get things their own way, if your back is against a wall, you really want a Motivator fighting in your corner, especially if there is no other way of resolving the problem other than via a direct confrontation.

Most of the modern world's business, religious and political leaders have strong Motivator personality traits – but these characteristics are latent in all of us, and can be developed and utilized by everyone.

POSITIVE TRAITS ASSOCIATED WITH MOTIVATION:

The building block of MOTIVATION can give each of us the following abilities and characteristics:

- Good boundaries
- Healthy assertiveness
- Aggressive self-protection
- Courage
- Leadership
- Personal self-discipline
- Incredible determination – even against all odds
- Can resolve problems with sheer grit, refusal to give up or back down
- Easily inspires others
- The ability to wield a lot of influence in the world
- Charismatic
- Can provide the 'spark' that leads to change / transformation
- High energy
- Passionate

BUILDING BLOCK 2: CONNECTION

The second of the four fundamental building blocks of the human psyche is CONNECTION. Connection manifests itself in a number of different ways. Internally, CONNECTION needs to occur between our synapses and between different pieces of information to draw the right conclusions and come up with new insights when presented with raw data or different types of information.

When people have a lot of CONNECTION in their personalities, they will often be extremely fast, agile thinkers, able to make the sort of creative connections that are often described as 'genius'.

Connecting one thing to another often results in creating a unique or different perspective, but connecting to too many things at once, or trying to connect things together that really have no place together, can quickly lead to overload, anxiety and overwhelm.

The essence of CONNECTION is bringing things together. Some element of CONNECTION is required in order to interact with the world, and with other people. CONNECTION is also the founding of good communication, which is the basis of transferring information from one person to another.

Connectors are often excellent gatherers and sharers of information, which combines their strong analytical ability with their ability to reach different people in a way that really speaks to each individual.

CONNECTION can't happen in a vacuum, it constantly requires something or someone to connect to. People with a strong CONNECTION component in their personalities are frequently restless and can find it hard to stay still, or remain focused on one thing at a time.

CONNECTION thrives on making new connections, and so is always seeking movement both in its environment, in its thought processes and in its experiences and relationships. CONNECTION is naturally drawn to travel, fast-paced action, and thrill-seeking, which can quickly spiral out of control in an unbalanced state. Be warned that 'fast thinking' can often lead to breakdowns, as well as breakthroughs.

Although Connectors typically lack the intense charisma and drama of Motivators, they can still get things moving. Where MOTIVATION is the energy of transformation, CONNECTION is the energy of transportation, moving things along, moving things around, and bringing people and information together. But CONNECTION's energy is usually far less combustible or dangerous than the type of transformational events that can occur with MOTIVATION.

CONNECTION can be a restless energy, but when it's properly tapped-into and harnessed, Connectors can be some of the most productive and industrious people on the planet. Some Connectors will dutifully and methodically fulfill their tasks like the proverbial windmill whose sails are constantly turning. Other Connectors operate with the force of a hurricane, blowing through problems and issues and work before taking off for a change of scenery or a new project.

When the urge to Connect is thwarted, it can keep a person going round and round in circles, obsessed with doing things perfectly, or compelled to keep revisiting the same action, reaction or thoughts, endlessly and anxiously going over things again and again. Excessive CONNECTION can quickly lead to overwhelm, anxiety and burn out. When it's unbalanced, the urge to Connect can also degenerate into promiscuity, frivolity and thrill-seeking just for its own sake.

The Connector has a tendency to run away into work, or shopping, or busy-ness, and will often be trying to multi-task instead of just giving each project, each situation, each person, their own time and space.

Connectors are the most restless and busy of all the personality types. Connectors can feel constantly driven, constantly searching for more, for different, for new.

Connectors typically dislike confrontation, and whenever they come up against a 'brick wall', they will prefer to find a way around it rather than trying to blow it down. Connectors also rarely like to tackle issues or problems head-on, preferring to avoid serious conversations and delay big decisions as much as possible.

The life of a Connector is typically chock-full of working, shopping, holidaying, thinking, exercising and doing, and the main emphasis is on DOING, which leaves relatively little time left over for BEING. Perhaps, ironically, the constant rushing around and busyness can make it difficult to forge a deeper relationship with Connectors.

Connectors can find the idea of BEING, of spending quiet time thinking about deeper ideas related to the inner dimension of life, disturbing to the point of almost being painful. Connectors are usually aware when there is a problem or issue, but they often don't want to have to face it.

When they're under stress, many Connectors find themselves dealing with a powerful need to have a change of scene, whether it's changing their residence, job, or partner. Many Connectors are serial holiday goers, and will plan their holidays carefully for months and even years in advance, to ensure they have the least possible amount of 'down' time. Connectors can also be serial daters, never quite ready to settle down and commit to just one person.

Connectors can sometimes struggle with the concept of taking responsibility, preferring to run away from the mess they've made and the debts they've run up and the people they've hurt, than to try and clear it up. This can be a particular problem for an unbalanced Motivator-Connector, who can sometimes combine lack of responsibility with a selfish emphasis on putting themselves first and 'using' others for their own ends.

However, a balanced Connector can stay anchored in their obligations and responsibilities, thanks to their feelings of love and consideration for others, or due to their more idealist view of how people should behave.

Connectors are often very personable and easy going with other people, and can happily 'go with the flow', while still coming across as very genuine. Some Connectors (the Connector-Philosophers) are capable of an obsessive attention to detail, which can see them researching a topic minutely, or obsessing over a piece of work for days, until it's completed properly.

But in contrast to Philosopher types who get their wisdom and insight from deep contemplation and creative intuition and problem solving, and Motivators, who work via flashes of inspiration, Connectors tend to get their knowledge from fact-gathering, research and hard work. Their wisdom-gathering ability is much more linear than typically found by Motivators and Philosophers, and so tends to be much easier to replicate and to teach others.

Connectors excel at process, and at connecting disparate bits of information together. Evolved Connectors tend to be fast-thinkers, and intellectually very smart. They are often the 'power behind the throne', letting the more flamboyant Motivator personalities front the operation while they're happy pulling the strings invisibly from the back.

Connectors are often the most socially at ease of all the personality types, able to flit easily from one social group or one conversation to another. A balanced Connector can often introduce a new viewpoint to a discussion, or add information that will help to clarify where the truth lies, but they do so in a gentle way where the focus is on sharing knowledge as opposed to browbeating others into agreeing with them.

Where Philosophers have a tendency to be deep and heavy, Connectors are often light and airy, skipping over things that a Philosopher can easily get stuck on. Connectors tend to have shallow but very broad knowledge, which means they can usually find something to talk about with just about anyone.

While Connectors can often see the bigger picture, they lack the Philosopher's idealism and the Motivator's courage and determination to really do anything notable with that information. Connectors often find themselves partnering up with Motivators as the 'brains', or the 'fixers' behind the scenes, both for the good and for the bad.

But Connectors and Builders can make for awkward roommates and can struggle to find common ground, particularly if in the unbalanced state. The Builder's 'surface nice' and stability can irritate a curious and restless Connector, whilst reliable Builders often conclude that there's no point investing in a Connector who is here today and gone tomorrow.

POSITIVE TRAITS ASSOCIATED WITH CONNECTION:

- Innovative
- Creates synergy
- Knows when to back off
- Avoids unnecessary confrontation
- Industrious

- Has know-how
- Thinks methodically
- Intelligent
- Fast learner
- High energy
- Good problem-solver
- Fun
- Can lighten things up
- Gregarious
- Social connectors
- Friendly
- Good communicators

BUILDING BLOCK 3: PHILOSOPHICAL THINKING

The third building block of the human personality is PHILOSOPHICAL THINKING, which is defined as the ability to really think deeply about things and to deeply contemplate and observe circumstances and situations before drawing conclusions about what is happening, and why, and what that might mean for the future.

Where MOTIVATION is the power of transforming the surroundings, and CONNECTION is the power of movement, PHILOSOPHICAL THINKING is the power of changing the self. PHILOSOPHICAL THINKING is the building block most associated with self-awareness and truthful, unflinching evaluation of the circumstances in which a person finds themselves.

PHILOSOPHICAL THINKING enables people to adapt to the reality of their environment even when that means they may have to make decisions that will lead them into increased isolation, or to appear 'weird' and like a non-conformist to others. While PHILOSOPHICAL THINKING lacks the obvious dynamism of MOTIVATION and the furious, rushing pace of CONNECTION, Philosophers can often penetrate deeply into places, problems and mysteries where no one else can reach.

In its balanced and developed state, PHILOSOPHICAL THINKING is the energy of deep insight and idealism. Philosopher personalities are often happiest opting out of the rat race and spending their time in a place of calm contemplation where they can peel away the layers, or untie all the knots of a thorny problem, dilemma or decision in their quest for truth, clarity and justice.

PHILOSOPHICAL THINKING can't be rushed, but that doesn't necessarily mean that Philosopher personalities move slowly, especially when they are being blocked or dammed in some way. Then, a tremendous force can start to build up behind the obstacle until the obstacle is dislodged and the Philosopher sweeps away all before it, like a tsunami or a river bursting its banks.

When people have a lot of PHILOSOPHICAL THINKING in their personalities they can be viewed as unrealistic idealists or irrational troublemakers by others, and can appear to inhabit their own world of strange ideas and different ways of doing things.

PHILOSOPHICAL THINKING often suffers from the drawback of being too bitter and unpalatable to be easily accessed by others who don't naturally have a lot of this building block in their own personalities. It's true potential is usually only unlocked when it's transformed from bitter to sweet, making it easy for others to gain access to the wisdom, insight, or call to action it contains.

Philosophers tend to be the most innately creative and artistic of all the personality types, which is why so many singers, artists, writers and non-conformists often have a strong PHILOSOPHICAL THINKING streak in their personalities. Many Philosophers can't be held in place by the same societal norms the other personality types are working within. Philosopher personalities are typically off the beaten path, trying to forge their own path in life.

Philosophers will seek out new approaches and new ways of doing things, and can often come up with surprisingly innovative ways of solving problems by 'thinking outside of the box'. The Philosopher personality's creativity also enables them to adapt to extreme, strange and challenging circumstances.

Some Philosopher personalities can freeze in the face of difficult challenges and stressful relationships, which can descend into mental paralysis and depression if not checked at any stage. Other times, Philosophers can be subjected to such intense or fierce 'heat' from a devolved Motivator that they can disappear out of view and, as a result, drop all social interaction and/or personal contact with others. When this happens, the Philosopher can become very ungrounded and feel as though they are disconnected from themselves as well as from the world around them.

Due to their unyielding idealism, piercing insight into others, and quest for truth and justice, Philosophers can often antagonize Motivators. When Motivators go on the offensive, Connectors will flee, while Builder personalities will 'make nice', hoping to avoid any head-to-head confrontation and avoid the worst, the Philosopher personality often stands its ground. However, this type of thinking can be seriously mauled by the Motivator's aggression, often leading to the Philosopher wanting to withdraw from society again as a result of the encounter.

However, the more balanced Philosopher personalities can actually benefit from a pressured encounter with a Motivator, as it can help them focus their thoughts and go on to express themselves in a more articulate and charismatic way. Once the ideas have been 'tested' in the Motivator's arena, the Philosopher often finds it easier to share their wisdom and idealism in a way that is easier for the other personality types to access. But it's a trial by fire, and not every Philosopher personality can stand up in it.

However, despite the hardships and danger involved in challenging a strong, unbalanced Motivator, many Philosophers persist in seeing themselves as the 'antidote' to the worst excesses of a Motivator personality, despite the potentially great personal cost of confronting them.

Philosophers are typically the most 'alone' of all personality types. While selfish or anti-social behavior can also cause an unbalanced Motivator to spend a lot of time by themselves, their 'aloneness' is usually not by choice. By contrast, Philosophers often prefer their own company and actually need to spend a large amount of time alone in order to reflect, and renew and recharge their batteries.

Philosophers are deep thinkers and can often be very intense emotionally. Strong Philosophers aren't scared to dive into even the thorniest or trickiest of subjects, and to explore even the most controversial ideas, to really plumb the depths of the argument to see where it leads.

Philosophers can expend a lot of time, energy and effort on using their wisdom and insight to try to combat what they perceive as 'injustice' and 'unfairness' in the world, with mixed results. While a little truth and idealism can often go a long way to getting people to think a little differently, achieving the sort of 'global change' many Philosophers crave involves uprooting entrenched attitudes and vested interests that can usually only be challenged at great personal cost.

While Philosophers relish the idea of having a true meeting of minds, they typically plough a lonely furlough in life, as these meetings with kindred spirits are often relatively few and far between. But when two aligned Philosophers meet, this can develop into an extremely profound and rare friendship.

The Philosopher personality's main challenge lies in being able to find the common ground required to interact with the other personality types without submerging them, extinguishing them, or causing them to switch off and disconnect. Philosophers tend to get on best with other Philosophers, and also with Connectors, some of whom can often take the deep, novel ideas expressed by the Philosophers and run with them, dumbing them down enough in order to easily communicate them to others.

The Philosopher's deep contemplation often leads to idealistic, but unrealistic and impractical ideas about how the world should work, and how people should act and behave. When other people fail to live up to these theoretical, ideal states, Philosophers can become very judgmental and disappointed, often turning a cold shoulder to and freezing out those who have let them down.

Because the Philosopher personality's inner world is often so interesting and absorbing, they can often experience some difficulty when it comes to stepping out of their bubble to interact with other people on their terms. This can lead to Philosophers preferring to spend more time exploring their own inner dimension rather than engaging in social arrangements.

Philosophers can easily 'disappear' when things start to get too hot and stressful, withdrawing into their own thoughts and ideas, and often physically leaving the party to find a quiet spot where they can just be by themselves and think. The more unbalanced Philosopher personalities can spend a lot of time lost in the screen, or off in a book or a movie, underlining their preference for the imaginary world instead of the real one.

The Philosopher personality's penetrating insight often means they can see potential problems and issues more clearly and at a deeper level than others. Where others just notice the tip of an iceberg, the Philosopher is 15 leagues down trying to get a clear picture of the 9/10ths hidden under the surface.

In a stressed state, this superior knowledge can cause Philosophers to act in a condescending way, easily dismissing and disapproving of others because of their lack of awareness and idealism.

While Motivators can also try to hog the limelight, and build themselves up at other people's expense, there are a few notable differences between the two personality types. Firstly, while Motivators will openly try to convince others of their innate superiority, Philosophers typically don't blow their own trumpets in public, preferring to push the superiority of their *ideas*, aggressively, and often privately, or at one step removed.

When the Philosophy personality becomes arrogant, heavy or bitter, it loses a great deal of its usefulness in the world, as the other personality types are put off from engaging with the Philosopher's insights and ideas when they're expressed in such an unpalatable fashion.

The personality type which most benefits from its interactions with a balanced Philosopher – and vice-versa – is the Builder. With their pull to superficiality and materialism, Builder types can start to grow in all sorts of wonderful ways with some exposure to the depth and realness of a 'palatable' Philosopher. On the other side of the equation, the Builder personality can help to ground the Philosopher and turn their high ideas into practical benefits and applications.

That said, if the Philosopher spends too much time interacting with unbalanced Builders, they can become quite miserable and disorientated by what they perceive as excessive materialism and superficiality. Superficial settings make it hard for Philosopher personalities to keep their crystal clear clarity and focus, but these interactions are very useful in teaching the Philosopher personalities what ideas and principles it might need to jettison if it really wants to make its mark in the world.

Because Philosophers are happy to spend a lot of time alone, much of their self-expression occurs at a remove, for example via their art, their painting, and their writing, as opposed to directly in person. Philosopher personalities like to cast a pebble in the ideological pond and watch the ripples spread out.

However, if Philosophers spend too much time in their own company, online, or lost in their heads, they can start to stagnate and lose a lot of their creativity and inner luxuriance. To avoid stagnating, the Philosopher has to be careful to keep moving and exploring, and to not get stuck in one place.

Communicators can often prove very helpful to Philosophers by helping them break up stagnant ideas and modes of expression, and by encouraging them to connect to different people and different ways of doing things.

POSITIVE TRAITS ASSOCIATED WITH PHILOSOPHICAL THINKING:

- Truth-seekers
- Idealistic
- Justice 'warriors'
- Realistic
- Resilient

- Reflective
- Can accurately assess situations and people
- Patient
- Aware
- Peaceful
- Principled
- Authentic
- Insightful
- Deep
- Can resolve complex problems by deep, creative thought, thinking out of the box

BUILDING BLOCK 4: BUILDING

The fourth and last personality building block is BUILDING. The ability to manifest things tangibly in the world provides the support for the other building blocks to express themselves. While the value of 'doing' is often considered to be menial and cheap, the tangible benefits of 'doing' are often the most highly valued and enjoyed. Think of the illegal immigrants who are often drafted in for slave wages to build a multi-million dollar home or apartment building; or the poorly-paid sewing machinists who create designer clothes; or the production line workers in a factory that turns out high-end sports cars.

So, BUILDING is subject to a strange dichotomy where its outcome is highly valued but its process is often denigrated and unappreciated. But the truth of the matter is that without engaging in some sort of BUILDING, it's very hard to bring potential into actuality.

People with a strong BUILDING component to their personalities are often bountiful and giving, but will often engage in most of their interactions at a strictly superficial, surface level. But for those willing and able to make the effort to dig deeper, and who have the patience to explore further, BUILDING personalities can often reward them with a wealth of treasure, precious stones and pure gold.

Builder personalities tend to be the dependable, stable people that keep daily life functioning and ticking-over. Builders are often extremely solicitous about other people's well-being, and will naturally put themselves out for others more than any other personality type. They like to do favors for others, and they try very hard to keep the peace – tendencies which can make them very easily exploited by others if the Builder personality isn't balanced enough to protect itself properly.

Builders tend to be more focused on what they can do for others, and less focused on what others can do for them. They can be very generous and kind, producing whatever they're asked for or relied upon to do. Unlike impulsive Motivators, unreliable Connectors and absent-minded Philosophers, Builders are typically solid, reliable and predictable.

Lacking the Motivator's flamboyancy and attention-seeking, and with a pronounced sense of loyalty which is often lacking in the Connectors, Builders are in it for the long-term, whatever 'it' happens to be.

Operating in the background and behind the scenes, they tend to be much more accepting of others than the other personalities, and less judgmental. This can make Builders very easy to get along with, at least at the superficial level. Generally, they don't make a lot of demands and they will put up with a lot of bad behavior, selfishness and even abuse from others – which can potentially leave them wide open to being treated very badly.

Builders can have a very low opinion of themselves, and in the more extreme situations, can view themselves as being worthless, and having no intrinsic value beyond what they do for others. They often measure their true value by how much they are 'producing' or giving to other people – i.e. how many favors they do, how much help they are providing, or how dependably they show up to other people's parties, etc.

If they don't feel they are helping other people enough, they can start to feel bad, or guilty, and they also spend a lot of time struggling to overcome a sense that they've done something wrong, without being able to identify what it is, exactly.

These tendencies can make it easy for other stressed personality types, especially Motivators, to manipulate Builders and guilt them into doing what they want them to do. While it can seem that the dominating Motivator is totally to blame for holding the Builder personality captive, the truth is that the Builder also shares some responsibility for getting caught in these unbalanced relationships.

That's because Builders can lack the natural boundaries found in the other personality types. The Builder personality often believes they have to be available, all the time, to anyone who wants or needs them. They will passively go along with other people's plans instead of making their own, and will often slide into any role that's assigned to them.

This is how they can end up as the 'slave' of a Motivator, the therapist of a Connector, and the cheerleader for a Philosopher. But this can come at the cost of never really being 'there' for themselves, or knowing what they themselves really want, or prefer, or like. While Philosophers feel responsible for solving humanity's problems at the theoretical and global level, Builders feel responsible for taking care of everyone's issues on a daily basis.

The Builder's biggest challenge is often learning to say 'no' to others, and to express what they really think. While this personality type often loves to give, they also have to remember that they can also get depleted and denuded over time if they are being over-worked, or aren't being treated properly.

Builders also need to rest occasionally, and to put the emphasis on nourishing *themselves*, in order to be able to continue giving to others in a healthy way. But they can often feel bad if they have to pull back and put themselves first. While balanced Connectors and Philosophers will usually respond positively to Builders needing a bit of time to themselves, an unbalanced Motivator can respond very negatively if they feel that a Builder relationship is slipping away from them. When this happens, unbalanced motivators can lash out with rage, precipitate guilt trips and employ angry manipulation tactics to try and bring the Builder back under control – often leaving the Builder personality shell-shocked by the ferocity of the attack.

As the most solid and dependable of the personality types, Builders can find themselves getting stuck and stagnating very easily. They lack the raw, transformational energy of MOTIVATION, the easy movement of CONNECTION, and the persistent idealism of PHILOSOPHICAL THINKING.

Builders can struggle to overcome a mighty big sense of inertia and heaviness that often encourages them to act lazy and pick the path of least resistance in life because it seems so hard to really be able to change things around or try something new.

It's not unusual for a Builder personality to take many long years before they are ready to really make a change, to take a relationship in a different direction, or to challenge the status quo – but when they *do* finally decide to take action, it can be experienced as a literal earthquake in the lives of those around them. Rare as they are, when these earthquakes happen, they can totally and permanently transform the whole landscape.

Builders tend to be the most superficial of the personality types, with most of life being spent on the surface, or at a very shallow level. That doesn't mean they don't possess depth, it's just that most Builders are so busy producing and giving to others, they usually haven't given any thought to how to access and develop their own hidden resources and deeper abilities.

It's not unusual for Builders to neglect their inner dimension, often to the point of becoming totally disconnected from their own true thoughts and feelings. This is where Builders can often benefit tremendously from a Philosopher's deep wisdom and insights – but only when it is presented in an accessible and easy-to-take in way. An unbalanced or stressed Philosopher can easily submerge the Builder personality with its strong view of things, leaving the Builder personality feeling very bogged down and unable to say what they really think.

While Builders can be badly burnt by an unbalanced Motivator, if they have the correct boundaries and protections in place, a healthy Motivator can provide Builders with the impetus and energy they need to start to grow and develop more of their innate abilities and gifts.

Builders tend to get on well with the more easy-going Connectors, but can struggle to move past interacting at the purely superficial level of relationship. Builders can become irritated with the Connector's lack of gravity and commitment, while Connectors can sometimes find Builders 'boring' and too down-to-earth.

Connectors like to move on and explore new things. But the tendency of Builders to permanently anchor themselves to a particular view point or way of life, which can be very hard for them to budge from, is also the tendency that makes them the most prone of all personalities to keep going with negative and damaging relationships.

As part of the process of becoming more balanced and productive, the Builder personality will need to focus on erecting proper boundaries and asserting themselves more in their interactions with others. Builders will also benefit tremendously from making a commitment to themselves to explore their own inner dimension more, and to gain more clarity about what they themselves really want in life.

POSITIVE TRAITS ASSOCIATED WITH BUILDING:

- Good listener
- Helps others
- Peacemaker
- Non-threatening
- Loves others
- Public service
- Fair
- Can solve problems by bringing the different sides together and acting as a bridge for different viewpoints
- Non-judgmental
- Accepting
- Practical
- Capable
- Hard-working

TAKE THE PEOPLE SMARTS QUIZ

Before we continue, if you haven't done so already, this is a good time to take the People Smarts Quiz to discover your personality typology. You can also take the quiz online at: **http://peoplesmartsbook.com/quiz**

Pick the answer that comes closest to describing you. If you really can't decide between two responses, pick both.

1. **I would describe myself as:**
    M: Confident and assertive
    C: Meticulous and fast-thinking
    P: Honest and principled
    B: Patient and hardworking

2. **I'm most happy when:**
    M: I'm the center of attention
    C: I'm trying something new
    P: I'm doing something creative
    B: I'm surrounded by the people I love

3. **I would describe my decision-making process as:**

   M: Fast and intuitive

   C: Calculated and detailed

   P: Principled and insightful

   B: Difficult and confused

4. **When I'm stressed, I tend to:**

   M: Blow up

   C: Feel panicked

   P: Shut down

   B: Feel bad

5. **When things go wrong, I tend to:**

   M: Blame others

   C: Blame the process

   P: Blame the universe

   B: Blame myself

6. **I relax by:**

   M: Going on holiday

   C: Working out

   P: Reading a book, or watching a show

   B: Spending time with friends and family

7. **I like to:**

   M: Tell other people what to do

   C: Tell other people how to do something correctly

   P: Tell other people to think for themselves

   B: Listen to other people's advice

8. **When I'm having a disagreement with someone else, I:**

   M: Won't stop until they concede my point

   C: Am happy to hear objective information that could change my mind

P: Get frustrated quickly, and give up

B: Try to see the other person's point of view

9. I am best at:

M: Inspiring others

C: Inventing new ways of doing things

P: Creating something from scratch

B: Making peace and helping others

10. I am often:

M: Intuitive

C: Analytical

P: Insightful

B: Easy-going

11. Other people might describe me as:

M: Bossy

C: Perfectionist

P: Judgmental

B: Weak

12. My thought process tends to be:

M: Decisive

C: Logical

P: Deep

B: Confused

13. I prefer to:

M: Lead others

C: Learn from others

P: Do things differently from others

B: Help others

14. I dislike:

M: Insubordination

C: Boredom

P: Injustice

B: Arguments

15. My relationships usually end up being:

M: Volatile, but intense

C: Numerous, but superficial

P: Few, but real

B: Stable, but challenging

16. I find it hardest to:

M: Apologize

C: Relax

P: Lighten up

B: Say 'no'

17. I prefer my interactions to be:

M: Dramatic and engaging

C: Intellectually-satisfying

P: Deep and meaningful

B: Light and practical

18. When I hit a difficulty, I usually react with:

M: Determination to overcome it

C: Thinking how to work around it

P: Giving up and retreating back into myself

B: Pretending it didn't happen, and putting a good face on it

19. The following term LEAST describes me:

M: People-pleasing

C: Relaxed

P: Superficial

B: Confrontational

20. I am most afraid of:

M: Being ignored

C: Being unprepared

P: Being corrupted

B: Being alone

21. If I was shipwrecked on a desert island, the first thing I would do is:

M: Rant about the people who got me into that mess

C: Build a raft to try to escape

P: Use the time to meditate and introspect

B: Build a bonfire to call for help

22. What quality do you most value in another person?

M: Helpfulness

C: Intelligence

P: Honesty

B: Friendliness

23. My idea of fun is:

M: Starring in a Broadway show

C: Learning how to wind-surf

P: Painting a picture

B: Buying something new

24. Which statement best describes you?

M: I don't give up easily

C: I get upset if I'm late

P: I do my own thing

B: I put other people first

25. I like to:

M: Talk about my opinions

C: Talk about my ideas

P: Talk about my feelings

B: Talk about other people's thoughts and feelings

26. When a relationship goes wrong, I tend to:

M: Blame the other person

C: Move on quickly

P: Spend weeks thinking about what really happened and what it all means

B: Feel guilty and make an effort to get it 'right' again

27. I have a lot of:

M: Passion

C: Ideas

P: Wisdom

B: Patience

28. I most care about my:

M: Appearance

C: Work

P: Knowledge

B: Home

29. Which saying do you most relate to:

M: Revenge is a dish best served cold

C: For the sake of a nail, the battle was lost

P: Even the longest journey begins with the first step

B: There's no place like home

30. I would like to have:

M: Fame

C: Wealth

P: Influence

B: A nice home

31. Which statement best describes you:

M: Attractive

C: Talkative

P: Reserved

P: Approachable

32. In discussions, I prefer to:

M: Challenge

C: Analyze

P: Withdraw

B: Listen

33. I would like others to relate to me as someone who is:

M: Important

C: Successful

P: Wise

B: Kind

34. I often react to problems by:

M: Complaining

C: Innovating

P: Disengaging

B: Compromising

35. The best thing about the internet is that:

M: It gives me a platform

C: It gives me information

P: It gives me an escape

B: It gives me a way to stay in touch

36. I tend to:

M: Take the initiative

C: Think outside the box

P: Think deeply before I speak

B: Make peace, instead of war

37. I find it hard to:

M: Let go

C: Sit still

P: Keep going

B: Get started

38. I crave:

M: Influence

C: Achievement

P: Deep wisdom

B: Consumer goods

39. I would describe myself as:

M: Optimistic

C: Realistic

P: Idealistic

B: Blank

40. On the social scene, I am often:

M: The life and soul of the party

C: The consummate guest

P: The first person to leave

B: The hostess with the mostess

INTERPRETING YOUR RESULTS:

To work out your main personality type, go back to your quiz results and see how many answers you have in each of the four categories. The category with the most responses is your 'primary' or dominant personality building block, while the category with the second highest number of responses is your secondary personality building block.

If you have more than 32 answers in one category, you should consider yourself a 'Pure' personality type in relation to the PEOPLE SMARTS SYSTEM of 16 personalities set out in the next chapter.

However, most of us tend to be an admixture of 2 or even 3 of the main personality building blocks. If your personality type doesn't sound accurate, read the other personality types for your dominant building block to see which one more closely describes you.

The more we react to life from a place of 'balance', the more we'll be able to dip into the traits associated with the non-dominant building blocks as, and when, we need to. Over time, this can create some significant, positive changes in our personalities, and particularly in how we handle situations of overwhelming stress.

The negative aspects of each of the 16 personality types described in the following chapter usually only come out when we're under stress. The more adept we get at identifying the true sources of our stress, and dealing with it appropriately, the less these 'negative' tendencies will come to the fore.

If stress is currently playing a huge role in your life, the negative descriptions for each personality type may sound more accurate than the positive – but be assured that all the positive aspects are still there, too, and they will start to blossom as you continue the process of getting more into balance and defusing your stress.

And the opposite is also true, that if you are fortunate enough to be living a life that's relatively free of overwhelming stress, the negative aspects of each personality type will rarely surface.

The last thing to note is that while many of the personality types sound similar and share many characteristics with each other, in practice, a 'Motivator-Connector' will act and react very differently to a 'Connector-Motivator', for example, depending on which building block is actually dominant.

THE 16 PERSONALITY TYPES

Now that you've learned about the four basic building blocks of the human personality, and hopefully taken the PEOPLE SMARTS SYSTEM personality quiz to find out which personality type you most closely resemble, it's time to set out the 16 Personality Types that are at the heart of the *People Smarts* System.

Before we continue, let's remind ourselves how we got here.

The 16 *People Smarts* Personality Types are built up from the four building blocks of personality that we covered in the last chapter, namely: MOTIVATION, CONNECTION, PHILOSOPHICAL THINKING and BUILDING. Those four building blocks are based on the ancient world's four elements of FIRE, AIR, WATER and EARTH, as well as on the four principal stress responses discovered by modern science, namely, FIGHT, FLIGHT, FREEZE and FLATTER.

The following diagram sets out the connections clearly:

MOTIVATION	=	FIRE	+	FIGHT
CONNECTION	=	AIR	+	FLIGHT
PHILOSOPHICAL THINKING	=	WATER	+	FREEZE
BUILDING	=	EARTH	+	FLATTER

In an unbalanced or stressed state, we can devolve back into one main 'building block', with its associated stress response. At the other end of the spectrum, if we've done an awful lot of hard work on ourselves, we will be able to access all four of the building blocks and choose which stress response to respond to challenges with, as required.

The goal of the PEOPLE SMARTS SYSTEM is to set out a path so each person can get their personality balanced and 'unstressed' and therefore tap into their true potential, really understand themselves, and start to resolve some of the issues that might have been derailing relationships and dreams so they can live a happy, fulfilled life.

The starting point for the process is to figure out which of the 16 personality types set out in this chapter most accurately describes you. So without any further ado, let's introduce them.

MOTIVATOR PERSONALITY TYPES

Type 1: Pure Motivator

Type 1, the **Pure Motivator** is actually fairly rare in the world. Pure Motivators are often counted in the ranks of Planet Earth's biggest trouble-makers and instigators of change. Often utterly fearless (at least externally), the Pure Motivator will say and do things no one else would even dream of.

Pure Motivators are incredibly powerful personalities, and rarely brook any arguments or disagreements, especially when they are in an unbalanced, or stressed, state. People are often drawn to Pure Motivators charisma and passion, but getting too close to a Pure Motivator is often a risky proposition.

That's because Pure Motivators can often find it very difficult to contain their emotions or channel their enormous reservoirs of inner strength appropriately, especially when stressed. Getting caught up in a Pure Motivator's storm, or rage fit, is not something most people will never forget, and in this state, the Pure Motivator can inflict some deep wounds, even upon the people they truly care for.

With their forceful personalities, inability to take 'no' for an answer, and often surprisingly deep spiritual side, **Pure Motivators** naturally gravitate towards leadership positions. On the positive side, they can change the course of history by becoming the leaders of civil rights movements, or finding some way to use their notoriety, money and success to challenge injustice and deprivation.

Most of Planet Earth's saints and visionaries were drawn from the ranks of the **Pure Motivator**.

On the negative side – which is often prevalent amongst **Pure Motivators** – they can become the dictators, mafia Godfathers, immoral politicians and aggressively self-focused entrepreneurs who don't hesitate to throw the moral rule book out the window if it means they can get more of what they want.

More than any of the other Motivator personalities, Type 1 is extremely careful about their honor. If they feel they aren't being given the proper respect and attention, they can relentlessly pursue the person who they perceive as mocking them or slighting them until they manage to bring them down and 'teach them a lesson'.

When Type 1 is unbalanced or stressed to an extreme, the **Pure Motivator** can become a rageaholic, picking fights and manufacturing justifications that will enable them to 'dump' their feelings of anger on other people.

Type 2: Motivator-Connectors:

Type 2, the **Motivator-Connector**, is often unstoppable. Nothing can get in the way of a Motivator personality that also excels at connecting to and communicating with other people. Motivator-Connectors are quick-thinking, fast-moving and hard to contain. Many Type 2s have a natural propensity for invention, coming up with new ideas, new ways of doing things, or creating new products as they combine the Motivator's dislike of following rules with the Connector's ability to see things from a different dimension.

Motivator-Connectors are heavily represented amongst the ranks of genius inventors, cutting-edge artists and highly successful business people, because MOTIVATION gives them the determination to keep going with the new ideas that result from making new CONNECTIONS until they blossom into something concrete. MOTIVATION also gives this personality type the strength to fight for their ideas to be taken seriously in the 'real world'.

Motivator-Connectors can keep blowing dying embers into life long after everyone else gave up and went home. Pugnacious problem-solvers, they will return to a problem again and again until they find a way to resolve it, especially if it's a matter of pride or honor.

Motivator-Connectors can be energizing, but also exhausting to be around, especially if they are stressed. They can get a party going like no-one else, and when they're in a good mood, their upbeat outlook and forward-looking vibe is infectious.

But Motivator-Connectors can also be prone to over-extending themselves and burning out. They can become so giddily enthusiastic about their own ideas or 'big vision' that they sometimes don't notice that the more practical and tangible aspects of their business, organization, or relationships are coming apart or failing to work as well as they like to tell other people. This tendency to exaggerate success and paint inspirational, but unrealistically rose-colored pictures can lead to immediate and disastrous collapse if the Motivator-Connector doesn't have a more practical Builder or realistic Philosopher to help ground them.

On the negative side, the unbridled and creative **Motivator-Connector** can burn through people and cash very quickly, consuming their resources and assets at a scary pace and leaving their surroundings in ashes before moving on to new pastures.

Because they have the Motivator's tendency to disrespect boundaries and rules, other people can experience a stressed Type 2 personality as aggressive fighters who are ruthless and often more than a little unscrupulous. The Motivator-Connector can end up making a lot enemies and hurting a lot of people's feelings.

In the stressed state, Motivator-Connectors can react to others with harsh criticism and impossible demands for perfection. Often harshly competitive, they often only play to win and can be very demanding and irritable with other people, especially those they feel have let them down.

Unlike the Pure Motivator, the Motivator-Connector will sometimes prefer to run away than to slug it out, particularly if they don't feel they have a good chance of winning any confrontation. While the Pure Motivator often achieves things with sheer grit, determination and the strength of their character, the Motivator-Connector is more interested in shortcuts, loopholes and hacks to achieve meaningful goals, fast – and often, they find them.

Type 3: Motivator-Philosopher

Type 3, the Motivator-Philosopher can be mercurial, sometimes switching from the enthusiasm and energy of MOTIVATION to the sullenness and despairing bad moods of PHILOSOPHICAL THINKING very quickly when their plans or efforts don't pan out as they hoped. Until this personality learns how to properly manage and channel their powerful emotions, the Motivator-Philosopher can end up living their life bouncing from one extreme state to another, which can be extremely challenging for the people around them – and extremely difficult to experience as the person going through it.

When Type 3 is in balance they can combine the Motivator's raw passion and social magnetism with the much deeper insight, self-awareness and idealism of the Philosopher to really achieve some great things in the world. Their innate pull to the realism and idealism of PHILOSOPHICAL THINKING can be used to tamp down the unhelpful extremes of wishful thinking and impulsive action that can dog the Motivator.

The more philosophical side can take the time to think things through clearly, and to chart a course of action that will enable the Motivator's passion and energy to be applied in the most useful and beneficial way. This can make the Motivator-Philosopher an extremely effective and fast problem solver, enabling them to pull some miraculous rabbits out of the hat even at short notice.

The Philosopher's self-reflection can also make the Motivator safer for others to be around by keeping its self-centered and sometimes unscrupulous tendencies in check, while still ensuring that MOTIVATION's passion and energy is channeled and applied appropriately, generously and helpfully. The balanced Motivator-Philosopher is still a fighter – but they will tend to fight far more for others, and far more for the ideals and justice than purely for themselves and their own narrow interests.

Accessing the Motivator's passion and 'righteous anger' can also help to flip the Philosopher out of a depressed, cynical or bitterly inactive state, and get them back on their feet, out of hibernation and interacting with the world again.

PHILOSOPHICAL THINKING enables this personality type to think deeply into things. When this is combined with MOTIVATION's natural intuition and flashes of insight into others, the resulting foresight can be almost preternaturally accurate and incisive.

Motivator-Philosopher can be extremely accurate, if often unforgiving, judges of character. When in balance, they will use this knowledge for good, while the unbalanced Type 3 can often be tempted to use their great insight into others for self-serving, manipulative ends.

Motivator-Philosophers are the most introverted of motivator personalities. In the balanced state, they can feel equally at home by themselves as when they are in a crowd of people. While Type 3 personalities still crave attention, and still want to be noticed, they're often more interested in their ideas and their contribution to the debate being noted, than in getting kudos for their appearance or obvious status symbols.

Like all motivators, Motivator-Philosophers can be extremely charismatic and interesting speakers, and they can also interact with others a lot around deep ideas and serious questions about the meaning of life. This personality is often disinterested in 'fluff' and small talk, and can sometimes prefer to clam-up than to waste their time discussing mundane things like the best type of coffee at Starbucks.

On the negative side, Type 3s can experience life as alternating between ups and downs, and black-or-white, with very little 'grey' in between. This occurs because the Motivator-Philosopher personality is essentially pulled in two radically different directions, exacerbated by the Motivator's intense emotions. This can make the stressed Motivator-Philosopher's reactions highly unpredictable.

When stressed, Type 3s can find themselves dealing with the extreme despair and cynicism of the Philosopher, which are then exacerbated by the Motivator's tendency toward dramatic self-expression. The Motivator-Philosopher's emotional let-down from an ideal not reached, or a goal not accomplished, can be extremely intense.

Because a stressed Type 3 can spend large chunks of their time 'frozen' and inactive, they can often bounce out of that state straight into a mad rush to make up for lost time and do all the things they missed out on when they were in a despairing, apathetic and frozen Philosopher state. With the Motivator's unbridled enthusiasm and lack of boundaries, they can overdo things very quickly, take on too much – and find themselves hitting the wall.

When this happens, the Motivator-Philosopher can slide back down into cynical disappointment as the ideal is not reached, or can't be maintained, and the cycle starts all over again.

In common with the other motivators, the Motivator-Philosopher likes a captive audience to share their ideas with, and isn't scared to debate an issue. When stressed or unbalanced, this personality type can act in a condescending way to others, secure in their belief that they inhabit 'the moral high ground' – and they often aren't shy to tell you that.

Like all Motivators, this personality type often has very high expectations which are often not so reasonable or realistic. When these expectations aren't met, this can trigger a torrent of contemptuous rage. When stressed, the Motivator-Philosopher can exhibit a pronounced tendency to put guilt trips on others.

Dissatisfaction can be a big challenge for all Motivator-Philosophers. In the stressed state, this can lead to harsh criticism against other people, and a feeling that whatever they do is never 'good enough'. In the balanced state, this sense of dissatisfaction can be parlayed into a more positive sense of motivation and an impulse to keep going, even though the end still hasn't been achieved yet.

Type 4: Motivator-Builder

Type 4, the Motivator-Builder personality, is one of the most effective, efficient and active of all the personality types. They can get an awful lot done quickly, and are typically blessed with some notable organizational abilities. That's because they combine MOTIVATION's energy, passion and vision, with BUILDING's grounded, practical nature, easy sociability, and ability to take a seed and cultivate it into a tree.

When this personality is in balance, it takes on the quality of being an iron fist in a velvet glove. The Motivator-Builder energy is one of uncompromising diplomacy. The Builder side furnishes the ability to relate to others and make room for them to express themselves honestly, while the Motivator's side ensures that this personality type is still tough enough to not be taken for a ride.

A balanced Motivator-Builder can use their keen social insight appropriately to know when they should be taking things up a notch to achieve their goal, or when they need to bank the flame and take the pressure off.

Motivator-Builders are adept at 'playing the game' extremely well, and often enjoy doing so, combining the Motivator's forceful ability to persuade, manipulate and cajole others into going along with them with the Builder's easy sociability and charm. They often aren't as intimidating as the other Motivator types, because the more threatening negatives associated with Motivators personalities are 'hidden' underground.

While Motivator-Builders usually get on better with the world around them than the other Motivators, their more hidden nature can make them much harder to deal with, in some ways, as it's often not clear what's really going on, or why. Even day-to-day interactions can become stressful and 'complicated' when you're dealing with someone who is clearly upset, but refuses to discuss why or what can be done to rectify the situation.

Motivator-Builders, of all the motivator types, are the most genuinely interested in developing a two-way relationship with other people and are often very friendly and helpful, even to casual acquaintances. A balanced Type 4 can listen as well as speak, and will also occasionally give way on an issue and put the other person's needs or views ahead of their own.

Motivator-Builders often love to chat, and excel on the social scene where they are often seen as being charismatic, genuinely nice, and a big success in their particular field.

With BUILDING's strong pull to keeping up superficial appearances, and MOTIVATION's emphasis on personal honor and respect, Motivator-Builders are the most easily embarrassed and offended of all the personality types, and they can often still feel the 'sting' of being embarrassed publically, even many decades later.

Motivator-Builders can struggle with the issue of not using their sincerely-meant kindnesses and favors as levers to coerce and manipulate others into doing what they want. Type 4 personalities are often totally convinced that they are only doing things 100% for others, and have little awareness that this is not always the case. Motivators generally find it very hard to accept another person's point of view, and Motivator-Builders are no exception to this rule. The only difference is that Motivator-Builders tend to be far more 'gentle' in how they express their disagreements.

When balanced, Motivator-Builders can be indefatigable, charming, generous and helpful, and won't take 'no' for an answer when it comes to trying to do something for their community, friends or family.

Unbalanced Motivator-Builders can make very convincing con men and scam artists, because part of them really does care about others and really is interested in what you have to say, which can encourage the people they interact with to trust them more deeply than they would another unbalanced Motivator personality. The warning signs are often camouflaged, which encourages people to draw much closer than they would to a different Motivator Type that is under stress.

That's why, paradoxically, a caring Motivator-Builder can do far more damage to those around them than the other Motivator personalities when reacting from a stressed state.

An unbalanced Motivator-Builder can keep smoldering resentments going underground for years, which can suddenly burst out of nowhere, but then just as quickly things can get smoothed over again.

This friendly / fierce dual aspect can often make an unbalanced Motivator-Builder the most head-wrecking personality type for others to be around since you never really know when the 'nice guy' will disappear.

CONNECTOR PERSONALITY TYPES:

Type 5: Pure Connector

Personality Type 5, the **Pure Connector** is characterized by a rush to move on, and to keep finding something 'new' to get their teeth into, giving **Pure Connectors** an unparalleled drive to work hard and achieve. The Pure Connector has hyper-activity at their core, and finds it almost impossible to stop or to sit still. When this energy is focused sharply on specific goals and managed properly, it creates 'A' students, brain surgeons and brilliant lawyers and business leaders.

Many **Pure Connectors** will find themselves drawn to being first-responders, or doing other jobs that require them to be permanently switched on and ready to leap into action at a moment's notice. Often, the Type 5 personality is addicted to an 'adrenaline high' and will look for ways to maintain the action and adventure even when they're off-duty.

Like all Connector personalities, **Pure Connectors** are normally avid news addicts and can fall into obsessively checking their news feeds and favorites sources of information even multiple times a day in anticipation of learning 'the latest'. They can also get obsessed with trying new things, and often take particular pride in being 'the first' to have the latest technology, or to introduce a new way of doing things.

The Pure Connector is one of the most high-energy personality types, and when in the balanced state, they can be extremely intelligent, sharp thinkers and extremely fast learners. Pure Connectors love to liberally share information and ideas, and they can usually gallop their way through prodigious amounts of information, sifting, synthesizing and forming connections to get it out there much faster than anyone else.

No one else can really keep up with the sheer brain power and non-stop energy of a balanced Pure Connector, which can sometimes lead to the people around them getting quickly burned out and exhausted. Pure Connectors abhor feeling 'bored', and if this isn't properly managed and balanced with learning more of the habits of the Philosopher personality type, they can easily fall into the trap of seeking constant stimulation, activity and thrill seeking to keep things exciting and 'busy'.

Under stress, an unbalanced Pure Connector may have to deal with rushing thoughts that can lead to obsession, or rushing actions that can lead to compulsion. A lot of this busyness is due to an underlying sense of worry and anxiety which all of the Connector personalities are prone to. A stressed Connector spends a lot of time trying to deflect and run away from sources of anxiety and stress, which can manifest in constantly switching jobs / relationships / lanes, and looking for external sources of stimulation, including substances.

Lacking the Motivator's ability to challenge a problem head on; the Philosopher's ability to sit and contemplate; and the Builder's inherent stability, the unbalanced **Pure Connector** is the most prone to escaping into the 'extreme' jet-setting lifestyle of the international executive to try to outrun the anxiety; or descending into the never-ending cycle of anxiety-fueled obsessive-compulsive behavior.

The **Pure Connector** typically finds it the hardest of all the personality types to slow down, take a breath, and really relax.

Type 6: The Connector-Motivator

Connector-Motivator personalities can be some of the most productive people on the planet. They combine CONNECTION'S ability to act and get things done fast and efficiently with MOTIVATION's focus on the goal, and passionate enthusiasm for the cause.

While they are less combustible and way more easy-going than their Motivator-Connector counterpart, this personality type can still tap into MOTIVATION's assertiveness and determination to knuckle down and do whatever is acquired to achieve their goals. Meanwhile, the CONNECTION element keeps things flexible and fluid, tempering the Motivator's often unhelpful rigidity. Type 6 also finds it easier to communicate their vision clearly to others and to bring people with them in their pursuit of a goal, instead of the go-it-alone tendency of the Motivator personalities.

This combination of traits can make Connector-Motivators excellent leaders in their field. Type 6 can stand up for themselves and be 'hard' when they have to, but because they still have the CONNECTOR's dislike of confrontation, they will only press the 'nuclear button' on very rare occasions, and only when they feel they have run out of options for talking things through and sorting them out.

MOTIVATION's self-interest and focus on attaining specific goals can also keep the Connector-Motivator committed to a task, a job or a situation long after the innovation-loving CONNECTION side would have lost interest, got bored, or been itching for something new – but only as long as the Connector-Motivator can clearly envision the rewards for taking the path they are walking down.

Of all the personality types the Connector-Motivator is the most susceptible to becoming addicted to an 'adrenaline high', and they will look for ways to get that 'buzz' in all areas of life. Connector-Motivators are heavily represented amongst the ranks of obsessive joggers and gym junkies, and you will often find them bungee jumping, black-run skiing, deep-sea diving and generally looking for action and adventure anywhere they can find it, in all areas of their life.

Connector-Motivators tend to be highly competitive, and will often have an obsessive attention to detail. However, Connector-Motivators are less likely to deliberately play dirty than a Motivator-Connector, especially if there will be an obvious 'victim' of their crime.

In the stressed state, the Connector-Motivator's quick thinking, fast moving and drive to achieve as much as possible in as short a time as possible can easily morph from restless overachievement to aimless thrill seeking and harsh perfectionism.

The more intellectual Connector-Motivators can become addicted to increasing knowledge, endlessly researching the perfect shade of off-white to paint their walls and agonizing over perfecting the smallest detail of their reports, or even something as simple as a recipe. In the unbalanced state, even the smallest and most human 'flaw' in their efforts can have a severely negative impact on a Connector-Motivator's mood – which of course, only tends to exacerbate their sense of stress.

If the Connector-Motivator's obsessive need to be the best and do the best becomes pronounced, this can create a paranoid sense that other people won't do the job properly, and can feed their underlying feelings of anxiety and worry.

The unbalanced Connector-Motivator often lives life in the fast-lane, and they can become compulsive risk-takers. Perhaps unsurprisingly, that also means they can easily get enmeshed in stimulating substance addiction. In common with the other Connector personalities, unbalanced Connector-Motivators can find it very hard to slow down, which means they run a high risk of burning out.

Type 7: The Connector-Philosopher

Personality Type 7, the Connector-Philosopher, can combine CONNECTION's energy, optimism and lightness with PHILOSOPHICAL THINKING's deep insight, 'realness' and fearlessness. While the gravitas of PHILOSOPHICAL THINKING keeps them grounded in a specific project or interaction, the traction of CONNECTION can still make sure that things move forward at a smart pace, without getting too bogged-down in philosophizing.

A Connector-Philosopher tends to think before they act. They like to explore their options and all the angles before deciding on a course of action, and they are often one of the most 'together' personality types. A balanced Connector-Philosopher knows roughly where they are heading in life, and also how they are planning to get there, and what they are trying to achieve.

PHILOSOPHICAL THINKING's foresight enables them to overcome the CONNECTION tendency to waste a lot of time on pointless and unfocused wild goose chases, and it also gives the Type 7 personality the strength they need to keep going, and to persevere when things aren't going so easily.

Meanwhile, their Connector side helps to 'lighten up' the Philosopher's tendency to overthink, and to get bogged-down in abstract theories, and also helps the Connector-Philosopher to communicate their ideas to others in a lighter and more appealing way, which broadens their reach and gets other more involved in their projects and discussions.

A balanced Connector-Philosopher often works very hard towards goals they really believe in, and they can be a lot of fun to be around. But they also know when to step back, take some time off, and try to re-evaluate how they're spending their time, and where all their efforts are taking them.

After this time-out, when they get to relax mentally and renew their clarity, the Connector-Philosopher can return to the fray ready and eager to give their all to the project or idea they happen to be working on.

When in the stressed state, the Connector-Philosopher can struggle to translate CONNECTION's energy to get things moving and transformed into positive progress and action in the real world. Instead, all that energy can get sucked into endless and repetitive mental over-analysis, and can also manifest itself as increased nervous tension, leaving the Connector-Philosopher feeling permanently jumpy, anxious and 'wired'. Connector-Philosophers can also find themselves running off at the mouth, blurting out things in a stream-of-consciousness fashion that they'd never share with others in a more balanced and calm state.

When stressed, Connector-Philosophers can find it hard to make a decision, as they use PHILOSOPHICAL THINKING's tendency to overdo the analytical side of things as a defense to deflect away from the unpleasant or potentially scary things that the stressed Connector side wants to run away from.

An unbalanced Connector-Philosopher can become so worried about the outcome that they get too scared and discouraged to even begin. This inactivity can feed the Connector's anxiety, and exacerbate the Philosopher's tendency to become depressed.

Like all the Connector personalities, overworking can be a real problem for the Connector-Philosophers, who often alternate between periods of intense overwork which end with collapse. Under stress, this personality can then enter a 'frozen' state where they become unresponsive and unable to cope until they regain some of the strength required to pick themselves up and start over again.

Until the personality learns how to balance this out, this cycle can repeat itself over and over again.

Mixing the Philosopher's tendency to spend a lot of time alone with the Connector's need for new technology and 'progress' can lead to a lot of Connector-Philosophers becoming the archetypal tech nerds who live their whole life 'online'. They are still energetically interacting, communicating and 'surfing', but everything has become virtual reality.

Unbalanced Connector-Philosophers often prefer to telecommute, tele-date, and can easily become addicted to their computers, spending an obscene amount of time online and 'connected'. Care needs to be taken that the 'pretend perfect' relationships found online don't totally replace real, but inevitably flawed relationships.

Type 8: Connector-Builders

In the balanced state, Connector-Builders are often some of the nicest and most popular people out there. They have the natural gregariousness and curiosity about the world shared by all Connectors, but they are anchored in reality by the Builder's solid respectability and stability.

A Connector-Builder will like to find out all about you – where you're from, who you know, what you do – and not just to satisfy a fleeting curiosity, but because they're genuinely interested in other people and in hearing about their experiences.

The Builder's tendency to care about others and to try to 'do good' balances out the Connector's predilection for taking off at the first sign of trouble, or a problem. Balanced Connector-Builders will stick around even when the going gets tough, and they will try to listen and sympathize before switching back into the lighter 'Connector' mode to try and take your mind off your misery with a crazy stunt or a last minute outing to somewhere unusual.

Connector-Builders often put a lot of effort into cultivating their relationships, but can still keep things spiced-up and interesting. Whenever there's the risk of a hum-drum or a soul-destroying mechanical routine creeping into life, the Connector-Builder will find a way of changing things up in a nice way.

Connector-Builders are the people who will fly half way across the world so they can burst out of your cake at a surprise party. They will leave unusual little notes in your lunch bag. They will find out what your dream holiday is and then obsessively research which of the 100 best safaris to take you on.

Their BUILDING dimension means that the Connector-Builder really does care what other people think, and they will pour an awful lot of their CONNECTION energy and 'magic' into trying to make the people around them happy. The Type 8 personality is stable in the areas they need to be – holding down a job and staying loyal in their relationships - but daring and exciting on the fringes so life never gets dull or boring.

Indefatigably optimistic, Connector-Builders rarely think about what could go wrong, and also rarely dig deeper for their true feelings or thoughts about things. As long as it's working in the 'now', they're happy, and prefer to not spend a lot of time thinking about tomorrow.

The main problems for an unbalanced Connector-Builder comes from their tendency to run away from reality, and their insistence on taking everything and everyone at face value – including themselves. This personality type is often used – and sometimes abused - as 'gophers' and assistants by others, because they can combine the CONNECTORs ability to get things done quickly and efficiently with the Builder's gentle nature and reluctance to stand up for themselves.

In the stressed state, the Builder's inability to say 'no', can combine with the Connector's obsessive and perfectionistic tendencies to produce an anxious, miserable and stressed workaholic.

When stressed, Connector-Builders tend to experience the most performance anxiety of all the personalities, because they are out there doing a lot, and they have CONNECTION's drive to want to do it perfectly. At the same time, they also have the Builder's preoccupation with how others are viewing them, and a tendency to feel bad and somehow 'not good enough' if they can't be all things to all people.

Connector-Builders are the people who work into the night to get a last-minute report done for their boss or, as a result of being unable to say 'no', will wake up 3 hours earlier than usual so they can take their friend to the airport and still not be late for work..

Unbalanced Connector-Builders can sometimes be very superficial, unwilling or unable to look within, and often using levity and humor to deflect the conversation away from anything they deem as being 'too serious.'

Connector-Builders often need a lot of reassurance and feedback that what they are doing is OK, and if they don't get it, they can come to feel their lives are meaningless. If that happens, they often look to take their mind off this deep feeling of anxiety and dissatisfaction by filling their days up with even more superficial activities and meaningless 'busyness' to try and distract themselves from a deep feeling of inadequacy and unhappiness. This can make a stressed Connector-Builder prone to experiencing crippling anxiety and panic attacks which they believe come out of 'no-where'.

PHILOSOPHICAL THINKER PERSONALITY TYPES:

Type 9: Pure Philosopher

Type 9, the **Pure Philosopher,** is the archetypal absent minded-professor. Pure Philosophers like their own company, and have such a deep and opulently imaginative inner world that it can be very hard to coax them out of their heads into interacting with the real world.

First and foremost, Type 9 is a thinker, and they can easily be lost in their thoughts, or their writing, or their creative self-expression for hours at a time, unaware of the hours passing. While Type 9 often has a great deal of knowledge and insight about the world in general, they can struggle to apply that wisdom practically, to real life.

Philosopher personalities are idealistic, and value ideas, truth and wisdom above all else. In the balanced state, the **Pure Philosopher** personality can apply themselves to trying to resolve some of the hardest situations or to find answers to some of the world's toughest questions.

Where Connector personalities often have a great deal of broad surface knowledge about many different subjects that enables them to make innovative and often unexpected synergies, the Pure Philosopher's intelligence often manifests itself in very deep, but very narrow knowledge. They often don't know much about, and don't give a hoot about, anything that is not 100% within their realm of interest, but they will know their own specialty backwards and forwards.

Whilst Philosophers usually don't try to foist their ideas on others – unless they have a pronounced MOTIVATION side – they will stubbornly defend them, especially against people who they perceive as not doing their homework properly. Pure philosophers dislike wasting their time in superficial or pointless discussions, and can sometimes be curt with others to the point of rudeness, if they feel their ideas or knowledge aren't being respected.

A Pure Philosopher will continue to tell the truth as they perceive it, even if it's unpopular, and is more likely than any other personality to sacrifice themselves for a higher ideal. While Type 9s don't make friends easily, when they do find a kindred spirit, the friendship will tend to be intense, as **Pure Philosophers** tend to form very deep and authentic connections to the rare, right people who can really understand them.

In the unbalanced state, the Pure Philosopher's calm consideration of, and detachment from, real life can devolve into a zero-energy state where the person feels lost and empty and has zero motivation to get out of bed and to really interact with the outside world.

They typically react to stress by disconnecting from the world around them and exist only in their own bubble. Of course, no-one else can follow them into their heads, so this can be extremely lonely for the people around them. In this state Type 9 personalities can find it hard to really care about anything, as they find life meaningless and pointless. At its extreme, this stressed state can see the Pure Philosopher struggling to motivate themselves for even the most basic self-care, like showering and brushing teeth.

Under stress, this personality's "numbed-out" contentment with life can easily morph into serious depression. Like the other Philosopher personalities, Pure Philosophers can become easily addicted to their screens, which provides them with an easy avenue to 'escape' out of the real world and disconnect from it's very real problems.

Type 10: The Philosopher-Motivator

Personality Type 10, the Philosopher-Motivator, combines PHILOSOPHICAL THINKING'S deep insight and knowledge about what needs to change and improve in the world with MOTIVATION's ability to transform the environment and convince others that change really does need to happen.

When in balance, the Philosopher's self-awareness helps to keep a lid on the Motivator's power and determination and makes sure that it's carefully controlled, laser-focused and aimed at helping the masses, not just the individual themselves.

Philosopher-Motivators can make tremendously inspirational leaders who inspire people with the poetry of their words and the beauty of their vision, as opposed to the scare tactics and demagoguery that can sometimes be the hallmarks of the Motivator personalities. In the Type 10 personality, the Philosopher's idealism manages to balance out the Motivator's tendency to grab the spotlight and turn all the attention they receive to their own ends.

Part of what makes the Philosopher-Motivator such a successful and quietly persuasive figure lies in the fact that they really don't want the job. They much prefer to be operating quietly behind the scenes, and can often resent the amount of time a leadership role takes away from their own inner work and free-ranging thought process.

So, a Philosopher-Motivator will often only take on the role of 'leader' reluctantly, once they've been persuaded that there is no one better qualified to do the job. Once in position, however, they give it their all and take full responsibility for seeing things through to their conclusion. They can often act in very courageous and uplifting ways, which makes them adored by the masses, and tremendously respected.

Under stress, the Philosopher-Motivator personality can become bitterly and aggressively cynical, combining the often pessimistic, low-energy outlook of PHILOSOPHICAL THINKING with the anger of unbalanced MOTIVATION. Rage and disapproval against those who don't meet the unbalanced Philosopher-Motivator's high standards can be on a constant low simmer under the surface, but rarely expressed, even though it's consciously acknowledged.

While this personality type can sometimes secretly dislike other people for years, it will normally be expressed as a passive bitterness, as opposed to active vengeance. While the mood of a stressed Philosopher-Motivator can be pretty miserable, there's usually enough anger to keep them from plunging into the full-throated clinical depressions that can dog other Philosopher personalities.

If Philosopher-Motivators try to improve their lot in life but feel they don't get significant results, they tend to express their anger globally, at the world instead of individuals. Philosopher-Motivators can be scathing about other people's flaws, but more from a place of explaining why they want no part of the world, as opposed to the stressed Motivator-Philosopher's personal interest in making others feel 'small' so they can feel bigger in comparison.

Philosopher-Motivators often have an extremely sharp, but dark, sense of humor.

Type 11: Philosopher-Connectors

When Type 10, the Philosopher-Connector is in balance, the CONNECTION element is able to radically lighten-up PHILOSOPHICAL THINKING's penchant for getting a little too heavy and serious about life, and it can also stop the Philosopher-Connector from taking themselves too seriously and becoming a little pompous.

Philosopher-Connectors can strive after big ideas and idealistic visions and still spend a lot of time thinking about what life is really all about. They won't get stuck in a doom-and-gloom mindset and can still laugh at themselves – and the world.

The Type 10 personality is the most sociable of all the Philosopher personalities, often using CONNECTION's gift of communicating to share some deep ideas that would otherwise be phrased in a more heavy, philosophical way that most other people simply can't relate to. A balanced Philosopher-Connector can float new ideas in a way that will appeal to others, and then be able to translate that 'buy in' into some real traction in the world.

The CONNECTION dimension brings out the Philosopher's more fun side, and encourages them to step off their lotus pad and let their hair down a little. While Philosopher personalities can sometimes find the 'lightness' and 'superficiality' of the other personalities a little grating, Philosopher-Connectors tend to be the least disapproving and the most accepting of all the Philosopher personalities. This can make this personality type an excellent 'bridge' between the deep, internal world of PHILOSOPHICAL THINKING, and the more gregarious, social and expansive world of CONNECTION.

Under stress, PHILOSOPHICAL THINKING's propensity to get down and discouraged, and too 'inward focused', can be exacerbated into a vortex of despair. PHILOSOPHICAL THINKING and CONNECTION can combine to create a whirlpool of anxiety and depressed thinking, which at its most extreme can suck a person down to the very depths. Once this cycle of negative thinking, anxiety-inducing worry, and depressed rumination begins, it can be very hard to escape from.

Other issues encountered by an unbalanced Philosopher-Connector can be a tendency to tune people out. This combines the Philosopher's tendency to daydream and to withdraw from the real world with the Connector's anxiety-fueled lack of focus and inability to take in new information when there are already too many other thoughts crowding around and taking up all the bandwidth.

Practically, this can lead to a stressed Philosopher-Connector finding it hard to focus and engage with what people are saying to them if it's not something they really want to hear. This can take the form of selective memory, where they don't pay enough attention to things that are objectively important and really matter.

This tendency to 'blank' conversations can make this personality type notoriously unreliable when under stress, and can hold them back from being taken seriously in their chosen career or other endeavors where their lack of focus and 'sharpness' makes it hard for other people to trust them with important matters.

Sometimes, Philosopher-Connectors can get discouraged at the first hint of trouble or challenge and will want to give up. They can find it hard to stay the course, lacking MOTIVATION's ability to keep going and BUILDING's stoic acceptance, and then they will look for excuses to enable them to opt-out and go back to the safe environment of their bubble.

When unbalanced, this personality type can fall prey to the Philosopher's apathy and lack of excitement combined with CONNECTION's avoidance of tackling the real issues they face. When this happens, they can give up on themselves and their chances of changes things for the better, and can increasingly feel as though they just want to be left alone. They still have the Connector's need to interact and communicate, however, but they will tend to limit their social activities to impersonal or anonymous interactions online.

Philosopher-Connectors who get stuck in the negative state often find other people's expectations of them burdensome and heavy, and also resent being given 'superficial' advice on how to improve their lot in life.

Type 12: Philosopher-Builders

Type 12, the Philosopher-Builder, has the potential to become one of the most truly productive personalities. When it's in balance, the Type 12 personality can combine PHILOSOPHICAL THINKING's idealism, deep insight and creative ideas for how to do things different and better with BUILDING's grounded ability to actually get going and make it happen.

The Philosopher-Builder is often found leading an Non-Governmental Organisation (NGO), or spearheading a charity or organization that is actively trying to make a difference in the world. They are often also drawn to the teaching profession, where they put a lot of effort into nurturing their students and helping them to 'grow' and develop in every sense of the word.

Philosopher-Builders can also thrive in the area of practical research and invention where they can apply PHILOSOPHICAL THINKING's ability to really get to the bottom of a subject with BUILDING's focus on creating something constructive from the process and turning abstract ideas into tangible inventions and ideas that can really benefit people.

Often highly altruistic and generous to others, a balanced Philosopher-Builder is highly prized as a friend and partner. They can deal with other people's pain and hurt, but their more practical and optimistic side prevents these conversations from deteriorating into a never-ending 'pity party'. Philosopher-Builders will let people cry on their shoulder when they need to, but they don't want to get bogged down in misery, and are often adept at knowing when to 'pull the mask' back on and encourage others to pull up their socks and get back to the business of life.

This is true for themselves, too. Philosopher-Builders can often express some profound thoughts and feelings, but without getting 'stuck' in that heavy place for too long, to the point where others can find it weird or uncomfortable, and want to bail out of the conversation, or relationship.

When in balance, Philosopher-Builders are able to regroup from setbacks and difficulties. They can retreat into themselves and re-evaluate their priorities and abilities without starting to beat themselves up and feel like a failure. But they won't stay stuck in that contemplative place for too long, as the Builder gets them back on their feet and doing something constructive to use their new insights in a positive way.

When under stress, the Philosopher-Builder is the personality type who is most at risk for being 'persuaded' to begin taking anti-depressants and follow a medical course of action that they haven't personally bought into to keep significant others reassured that 'everything is OK'.

An unbalanced Philosopher-Builder can struggle with the Philosopher's clarity and realism about all the things that are really going wrong in the world – and in their life. And at the same time, they can also struggle with the Builder's tendency to just keep putting a good face on things and maintain a superficially 'perfect' appearance that life is still great and wonderful.

It can be a killer combination, and that's why anti-depressants and other medications can be so appealing to a stressed Philosopher-Builder who can often see no other way of being able to continue to function 'in this world' while being buffeted by such intense negative feelings.

Like all Philosopher personalities, Philosopher-Builders often have to deal with some very deep sadness and disappointment, often caused by the yawning chasm between how things actually are, and how they'd like them to be. Philosopher personalities have high standards of behavior that are often not so realistic and impossible to maintain over the long term.

Falling and failing are an inevitable part of life, but a stressed Philosopher-Builder can take life's inevitable bumps and setbacks very hard. This personality type is particularly prone to wearing themselves out trying to maintain an ideal, and / or keep everyone happy, until they hit their inevitable limit and can't do it anymore.

If they get caught in BUILDING's inability to truly express their deepest feelings to their nearest and dearest – and often, also to themselves – the unbalanced Philosopher-Builder can then fall into a profoundly depressed state.

All introspective Philosopher personalities can experience social anxiety if they feel like a fish out of water, particularly when they're forced into superficial, aggressive or overwhelmingly social environments. However, the Philosopher-Builder can have the most intense feelings of social anxiety, because their more superficial, BUILDING side actually wants to be able to participate in social events successfully.

So when a Philosopher-Builder can't perform as well as they'd ideally like to, they feel tremendous shame and embarrassment, and sometimes this causes them to avoid social interactions in the future to keep from having the same thing happen again.

BUILDER PERSONALITY TYPES:

Type 13: Pure Builder

When balanced, Type 13, the Pure Builder, is the archetypal 'salt of the earth' personality. Dependable, reliable, self-sacrificing and frequently very generous with their time, attention and effort, Pure Builders are often a boon for the people in their lives.

Pure Builders typically don't expect or seek a lot for themselves. They typically dislike controversy for its own sake and tend to avoid disagreements or taking a 'strong stand' on a subject, preferring to keep their interactions with others as light and superficial as possible.

Pure Builders often pride themselves on their reliability and stability, and resist being rushed or pushed into making what they perceive to be hasty decisions, or rash changes. The Pure Builder can feel very responsible for other people's experiences, and will selflessly help other people out to the best of their abilities.

In a balanced state, Pure Builders are uncomplicated and undemanding, and enjoy the simple pleasures of life like a good meal and a warm bath. They like structure and routine, and once they find something that suits them, it's very hard to pry them away or get them to try something new or different.

The Pure Builder's motto could be summed up as: If it ain't broke, don't fix it.

They often have sunny, friendly dispositions, and are happy to roll up their sleeves and get to work. The Pure Builder delights in being part of a team. He will be the guy at the base of the pyramid holding the whole edifice steady while others climb up and on to his shoulders.

When balanced, the Pure Builder will know themselves well enough to be aware of their limitations, enabling them to say 'no' without feeling guilty and without being taken advantage of.

However, sometimes their easy-going and kind nature can make it hard for the Pure Builder to really develop a true sense of self, and they can be all too easily swayed by what others say and think. Lacking MOTIVATION's sharp focus, CONNECTION's quick thinking and PHILOSOPHICAL THINKING's insights and idealism, Builders can often find it difficult to act alone or exercise independent thought without seeking permission from others.

Whilst they can express strong preferences about practical issues like what to have for supper or the best way to fix a blown fuse, Pure Builders tend to steer clear of expressing strong opinions about more abstract ideas or deep emotions, preferring to go along with the consensus opinion.

Like all Builder personalities, Pure Builders can rarely be persuaded to rock the boat.

In the stressed state, the Pure Builder personality can find themselves constantly playing a part and acting the way they believe others want. They can become so focused on trying to get along with others and get others to like them that they lose themselves and end up in a place where they don't know what they truly think or feel.

This can lead to Pure Builders feeling 'invisible' in their relationships, even with those who are closest to them, and particularly if they are surrounded by strong Motivators or Philosophers who aren't scared to express their own ideas and opinions.

This can be a particular issue with unbalanced Motivators who are seeking a captive audience, and are happy to encourage the Pure Builder's unreasonable self-sacrifice and self-effacement if it means they can get their own way. Unbalanced Builder personalities can find themselves gravitating towards 'Motivator' types to provide some of the enthusiasm, passion and direction they feel they are lacking, but this type of unbalanced relationship can quickly become unhealthy, and even abusive, especially if the Pure Builder is unable to set firm boundaries.

Type 14: Builder-Motivators

When in balance, the Builder-Motivator personality has a unique ability to stand up for themselves, and for what's right - but without ruffling too many feathers. Their superb social skills and genuine good heartedness can combine with MOTIVATION's forthrightness to put a point across in a compelling way without making enemies by belaboring it or descending into personal insults and aggression in order to 'persuade' people to agree with them.

MOTIVATION gives this personality far more get-up-and-go and focused energy than the other Builder personality types. Builder-Motivators can become real pillars of the community, mobilizing people to come together behind a particular cause or aim while also being willing to personally do the hard work required to make that happen.

Incredibly sociable, Builder-Motivators tend to be the 'hostess with the mostess', reveling in being the center of attention for their guests, but still genuinely concerned that everyone is having a good time and not trying to hog all the limelight. Builder-Motivators are often very family and community orientated, and that is where their down-to-earth organizational abilities and genuine warmth and passion for people can really shine– but this personality has to be careful about not tipping over into the Motivator's tendency to dominate and bully people into doing things against their will.

Balanced Builder-Motivators can make very good mediators, combining BUILDING's ability to see other people's side and build bridges between two camps, with MOTIVATION's ability to clearly and fearlessly say what needs to be said.

In the balanced state, Builder-Motivators can use their MOTIVATION-derived passion and strength of personality to ensure they have appropriate boundaries to fend off any danger from predators, while the BUILDING side of their nature can use their kindness and natural empathy for others to keep MOTIVATION'S sometimes aggressive approach controlled and appropriate.

The Builder-Motivator can assert themselves more than the other Builder types. In the negative state, this can manifest as manipulative demands and passive-aggressive behavior.

An unbalanced Type 14 personality can combine BUILDING's preoccupation with keeping up appearances, lack of self-awareness and keeping things superficially 'friendly' with MOTIVATION's vanity, flamboyancy, and angry demands that things are done their own way.

But while an unbalanced Motivator-Builder will display far more open anger than a Builder-Motivator does when under stress, both types often react by trying to dominate or control others 'behind the scenes', manipulating people with their kindnesses, 'fixing' people with their good advice, and pressuring others into changing to become more 'acceptable'.

Unbalanced Builder-Motivators can easily become addicted to social media, spending hours online, which can gratify their social side with very little emotional investment. They can also get drawn into trying to garner attention online with catty comments and sharp putdowns that in real life they would never dream of saying to someone else in a million years.

Stressed Builder-Motivators can also become sticklers for political correctness, as the unbalanced Motivator seeks to try to dominate and control others for not being 'PC' enough, while the unbalanced Builder can try to browbeat others into keeping their true feelings and thoughts to themselves to avoid rocking the boat or making an awkward atmosphere.

Type 15: Builder-Connectors

Type 15, the Builder-Connector is amongst the most giving and generous of all the personalities, combining BUILDING's kind-heartedness and practical generosity with CONNECTION's easy-going playfulness and ability to 'soar up' and see the big picture.

Builder-Connectors are extremely gregarious, and many of them are the archetypal 'social butterfly', able to flit between different groups of people and find something in common with each. As such, they are extremely good social connectors and can effortlessly get along with very different groups of people.

When balanced, Builder-Connectors can combine the Builder's desire to give to and help others with the Connector's desire to move on to new pastures when a situation or relationship becomes unhealthy or negative. This personality type is more inclined to try new things than the other Builder personalities, and less likely to get stuck in a rut.

But CONNECTION's urge for new adventures is balanced out by BUILDING's stability and willingness to stay the course. So the Builder-Connector will try new things and go to new places, but only after they've thought about them for a while instead of just rushing head-long into whatever adventure or opportunity happens to show up.

Builder-Connectors can struggle to develop any real depth in their relationships, but they can often compensate for that by their openness and willingness to hear different opinions and to learn new things from others, even if they disagree with some aspects.

Sometimes, they can chafe at the responsibilities they've taken on (or been burdened with…) as part of their BUILDING aspects of concern and kindness for others. This can lead to them developing secret fantasies of running away from it all and catching the first plane to Barbados. But with typical Builder stoicism, they won't admit that to anyone else, or make any big effort to try to solve the issue.

In part, this is because Builder-Connectors are often hyper-allergic to confrontation, combining BUILDING's love of peace and emphasis on social status and 'getting along' with everyone, with CONNECTION's dislike of taking responsibility, and its tendency to 'run away' from problems instead of facing them down and dealing with them.

In the stressed state, Builder-Connectors can take on too much and then run out of energy to get it all done, which can cause them to start beating themselves up and feeling pretty bad about all the people they are letting down. In contrast to an unbalanced Connector-Builder – whose desire to bolt often overcomes their kindness and consideration for others – Builder-Connectors tend to stick around, even when the going gets tough.

Unbalanced Builder-Connectors can spend a lot of time engaged in superficial 'busyness' to keep their mind off their problems, and are often plagued by feelings of deep anxiety and panic. While Builder-Connectors are often highly efficient and practical, even they can become exhausted over time if they don't learn how to say 'no' to other people and prioritize their time better. This personality can end up spending a lot of their own time and energy trying to solve other people's problems, while pretending they have none of their own.

Perhaps unsurprisingly, a stressed Builder-Connector frequently feels confused and can find it hard to remember details, especially about conversations or issues that are unpleasant, or that could lead to some sort of conflict. This personality type can also become unreliable and flakey if they feel forced into going along with what other people want.

Type 16: Builder-Philosophers

Type 16, the Builder-Philosopher, typically feels a lot of responsibility for making things go OK in the world. When in balance, they spend a lot of time taking care of other people and putting themselves out – but from conscious choice, not as a default option.

Builder-Philosophers are capable of some extremely profound insight into themselves and into others – if they can only access it. They often excel as being an unthreatening shoulder to cry on, as their inner Philosopher gives them the depth required to move past the surface, while BUILDING's kindness and genuine interest about other people makes them approachable and easy to talk to.

Builder-Philosophers often have some profound insights, but can still ground their ideas and apply them practically to produce something tangible, useful, and often quite beautiful in the 'real world'.

Where the Philosopher-Builder personality can sometimes get more bogged-down in philosophizing about what needs to happen and so lack the energy to actually get things moving, a Builder-Philosopher will just get on and do it.

Some truly beautiful things can start to occur when the Builder's practical kindness and no-nonsense approach to life meets the Philosopher's deep thinking and idealism. Builder-Philosophers don't just have good ideas for fixing the world, they actually roll up their sleeves and put their plans into action.

The Builder-Philosopher often has access to deep emotions and intense feelings when alone, but would be embarrassed and wary of expressing any real emotion in public, especially if it's a 'negative' emotion. The chasm between the superficial outer and the profound inner can sometimes give this personality type a pronounced 'duel character'. Unlike the other BUILDING personalities, the Builder-Philosopher is never 100% comfortable in superficial, social circumstances, and will always be looking for more meaning in the mundane.

When under stress, the Type 16 personality can get really miserable, really fast. That happens when PHILOSOPHICAL THINKING's idealist vision of how things should be is taken to an unrealistic extreme, and then combined with BUILDING's difficulties with setting proper boundaries and their tendency to try to please others.

This can make the Builder-Philosopher extremely susceptible to feeling compelled to help or act out of a misplaced sense of duty, with the result that they force themselves to fulfill the obligations they feel they have towards others, however unreasonable they may be, and at whatever the cost personally. Because they find it very hard to say 'no' – and believe ideologically that they should be saying 'yes' as much as possible – Builder-Philosophers can get stuck with the jobs that no one else wants to do.

Spending too much time doing things that bring them very little joy and that feel meaningless can deplete the Builder-Philosopher's energy and joie de vivre, setting up a vicious cycle that can be very hard to escape from.

An unbalanced Builder-Philosopher is the personality type which is most prone to using illnesses as a 'respite' from all the unreasonable demands being placed on them. They don't want to rock the boat, yet PHILOSOPHICAL THINKING's deep awareness tells them something is really not right. Often, the easiest way for a Builder-Philosopher to get some time to themselves and put themselves first without feeling guilty is by getting sick.

Builder-Philosophers generally don't adopt the passive aggressive behavior of the Builder-Motivator, and they don't admit their negative feelings to themselves as openly as a Philosopher-Builder. Instead, they tend to focus more on keeping a good face on things while running themselves into the ground for other people in an uncomplaining fashion.

An unbalanced Builder-Philosopher can experience the most social anxiety of all the personality types, combining BUILDING's need for social status and superficial 'looking good' with PHILOSOPHICAL THINKING's perpetual feeling of not belonging. Even relatively minor experiences of social embarrassment or awkwardness can devastate this personality type and cause them to feel like they just want the ground to open up and swallow them.

Often, they take things to heart so much because the Builder-Philosopher frequently feels personally responsible for other people's bad moods and negative experiences, even when it really has nothing to do with them. They often find themselves apologizing to everyone about everything.

As the least externally aggressive and mobile of all the personality types, an unbalanced Builder-Philosopher can be easily abused by others, but often find it hard to break away. Until they learn more balance, they can spend a lot of time feeling guilty and selfish, especially if they are in a situation where they need to put their own needs ahead of others.

THE PERSONALITY UNDER STRESS

Now that we've set out the four main building blocks of personality and the 16 principle personality types, it's time to take the *People Smarts System* up to a whole different level. If you were paying attention, you might have noticed that many of the negative or unhelpful characteristics of the 16 personalities occur when people get stressed.

To put this another way, most people in the world would have far fewer relationship issues, meltdowns, depressive episodes, road-rage attacks and general problems and difficulties if they could somehow manage to limit the amount of time they spend operating out of a place of overwhelming stress.

So many people are taught to believe that their personalities – including all the stuff they don't like so much – is somehow carved in stone and permanently fixed in place. This is really unhelpful.

And it's not true.

The brain is plastic, which means that the way the brain reacts to stimuli can change over time, both for the good, and for the bad. Also, stress plays a profound role in shaping our personalities and guiding our reactions. A person who isn't overly-stressed will often act in a very different way than someone who is 'stressed out of their mind', literally.

What this means is that over time, everyone can learn how to take down their stress response by choosing the best reaction to their difficulties and challenges. But first, we have to have a realistic view of where the stress is coming from and what it's really doing to us before we can begin the work of changing our reaction to it. And that's what we're going to explore in this chapter.

In an ideal world, a baby would come into the world being appropriately loved and cared for from day one. Its caregivers would never scream at it, never leave it in a soiled diaper, never manipulate it emotionally, withhold attention, or slap it.

This won't come as news, I know, but *we don't live in an ideal world.* And it's not just us – nobody does! Even the most well-adjusted people in the world have had their own share of difficult experiences, traumatic interactions with others, and times in their life when they went through tremendous pressure, loneliness, upset or stress.

So, the first *People Smarts* lesson to learn about stress is that difficulties, challenges and suffering are an integral part of the human condition. Every human being walking around on planet earth has had their own share of heartache, even the people who look like they were born with a silver spoon in their mouths and who externally seem to have it all together.

Many years ago I found myself at a three day 'self-help' seminar in London's West End, where one of the exercises involved being randomly partnered with someone in the room and then spending five minutes in total silence, literally just staring at each other, trying to not look away. We weren't allowed to talk, or to move. The whole point of the exercise was just to meet someone's gaze, and hold it.

Man, I was dreading it. At that stage of my life I still had very low self-esteem, and with my uncool frizzy hair, fat bum and pretty bad dress sense, the thought of just *looking* at a total stranger was pretty intimidating. And then it got even worse, because the person I got partnered up with happened to be one of those slender, beautiful, blue-eyed blonde types with perfect hair, a posh accent and expensive designer pumps. Everything about the woman screamed 'Successful rich girl!!!' – and my heart sank to my stomach. She was everything I was *not*, and now I'd gotten stuck having to stare down the aristocratic beauty queen of the class for five minutes.

But a very strange thing started to happen as we stood toe to toe, looking each other in the eye. After about 10 seconds, the expensively-dressed beauty queen with the perfect styling buckled and started to cry. She literally couldn't look me in the face, and it was then that I learned one of the most powerful lessons of my life: you can't judge a person's life from the outside.

Sure, she looked like a million bucks, but it very quickly become obvious that my staring partner really didn't like herself very much despite her perfect appearance and obvious wealth. I realized that even though I don't dress so well and my hair is crazy and I'm a size 14 (on a good day…), this woman's emotional difficulties dwarfed my own.

It's important to stress this, because so often we get caught up in some unhelpful 'wishing' game where we wish we'd been brought up with different parents, in a different household, in a totally different way. We tell ourselves that *if only* we'd had the perfect childhood or different advantages that we believe other people had, all our problems would be solved.

Honestly?

We'd still have problems, they'd just be different ones.

And while hardship can often be an extremely harsh teacher, especially when we go through chronic trauma or neglect during childhood, it's only in those highly testing circumstances that a person's true inner power and strength starts to shine through.

Some of those people who truly transformed the world, like Gandhi, Nelson Mandela and Helen Keller didn't have a perfect childhood, anything but. If you take a closer look at any of the people who really made a big difference, you will nearly always find that their past experiences were anything but easy – and that's actually what made them who they are.

The key to turning all the 'grit' that everyone goes through into pearls – instead of getting buried in it - lies in understanding how all that stress, trauma and neglect hard-wired our brains, physiologically, to react to external stresses and triggers in a particular fashion.

The second *People Smarts* lesson is this: these physiological responses to stress are **body-based reactions.** Just like Pavlov trained his dogs to start salivating at the sound of a ringing bell by associating that bell with dinner time, the most primitive part of the human brain is also 'trained' to react in a certain way by repeatedly stressful or threatening situations.

In exactly the same way that this primitive part of our brain got 'trained' to react in unhelpful and extreme ways, it can also be 'trained' to act more reasonably and helpfully.

But first, we need to be clear about what's really happening, and why.

THE 4 FS

As I mentioned earlier, each of the four building blocks of personality in the People Smarts System is connected to one of the four main stress responses of FIGHT, FLIGHT, FREEZE and FLATTER that have been identified by modern science as the following diagram shows.

When under stress:

THE **MOTIVATOR** WILL USUALLY START TO **FIGHT**.

THE **CONNECTOR** WILL USUALLY GO INTO **FLIGHT**.

THE **PHILOSOPHER** WILL USUALLY GO INTO **FREEZE**.

THE **BUILDER** WILL USUALLY GO INTO **FLATTER**.

Again, let's remember that nine times out of ten, these are body-based, knee-jerk reactions to stress. Until and unless we start to figure out what's triggering the stress response, and why, it's going to be very hard for us to choose a different, more balanced or appropriate response to the challenges we come up against.

Before we continue, let's just try to define what each of these 'stress responses' is really referring to.

You've probably already heard of FIGHT or FLIGHT – where we either put up a fight in response to a challenge or 'attack', or where we try to run away from it. You can think of these two responses as being on the more 'active' side of the continuum, which is why they've generally tended to get a lot more attention from the psychologists and researchers.

On the more 'passive' side of the continuum, there's the FREEZE reaction, where we get so overwhelmed by perceived threat or danger to us that we shut down. When people experience a clinical depression, it's an extreme form of a FREEZE reaction.

And then there is the FLATTER response, which is the hardest of all the Four Fs to really recognize and understand. In a nutshell, the FLATTER response involves turning a blind eye to other people's bad behavior, going into denial about what's really occurring, and falling back into 'people pleasing' behavior to try and keep the dangerous person appeased.

SOMETIMES, THE FOUR FS ARE USEFUL

I don't want to give you the impression that the Four Fs are always and only bad news, because sometimes they are actually really useful. For example, if we're about to get run over by a bus, then it's really useful to have the **FLIGHT** stress response kick in and override our rational brain. **FLIGHT** instinctively takes over and gets the stress hormones and adrenalin pumping around our body so we can quickly sprint out of harm's way. But if we have the same reaction every time our spouse wants to talk about going on holiday? That's totally unhelpful.

Or, say someone jumps out of the bushes with a Samurai sword and starts charging towards us. Then it's totally wonderful to have our **FIGHT** stress response kick in so we can fight back and knock our attacker out cold. But if we're reacting like that to the guy who pushed in front of us at the mini-mart? That's totally unhelpful (and will probably land us in prison….)

Or let's say that a tiger gets loose from the local zoo and springs in through our office window. We can't run away fast enough to escape it, we can't fight it off with our bare hands, so now our **FREEZE** stress response will kick in and we'll drop comatose to the floor and play dead so the tiger will leave us alone. That's great! Doing so potentially saved our life. But if we're turning into a depressed zombie every time the cute guy fails to return our call, or we didn't get the promotion we were after at work? **FREEZING** is totally unhelpful.

Or, let's imagine we got invited to the home of a Third World Dictator with a nasty reputation for feeding the guests who displease him to his pet piranhas – and we can't get out of going. Then it would be totally appropriate for us to swallow down our own opinions and preferences and just to spend the whole night fawning over President Evil, flattering him about how cute he looks in that military outfit and how clever he is. But then, if we can't express ourselves honestly to our family or to our close friends? That's totally unhelpful.

What I'm trying to get at here is that sometimes the stress response is a sane and completely appropriate reaction to the circumstances we find ourselves in. If we are being physically or emotionally threatened, then fighting back and / or running away and / or going numb and / or sucking up is often the best thing we could possibly do.

The problems start to occur when we get stuck in an inappropriate, or over-reactive stress response, which means we react from that place of **FIGHT-FLIGHT-FREEZE-FLATTER** *inappropriately, and too much of the time.* Doing so usually happens as a result of going through some sort of major trauma. I'm not talking about a common or garden variety type of trauma here – life is full of those, and we all experience some sort of difficulty or 'trauma' every single day. I'm talking about something that feels like it's life-threatening in some way.

To put this in different words, trauma can be caused by all sorts of things, including:

- Difficult births
- Serious physical illnesses

- Divorce or major family conflict
- Financial problems
- All forms of verbal, physical, sexual and emotional abuse and neglect
- Chronic lack of sleep
- Chronic lack of exercise
- Nutrient and vitamin-poor diets
- Death of a close family member or friend

Plus, all the more 'dramatic' and obvious forms of trauma like terrorist attacks, car accidents, muggings and personal assaults, etc.[1]

To put it in a nutshell, most of us have been affected by some sort of traumatic circumstance at some point in our lives that may have had a profound impact on how we start interacting with, and reacting to, our environment and the people it contains.

HOW STRESS CAN AFFECT OUR PERSONALITY

Stay with me here, as this next part is absolutely crucial to developing the sort of People Smarts that can transform how you understand yourself, and how you relate to others.

Each of these Four Fs contain an awful lot of raw 'personality power' when properly controlled and applied. But when we're feeling very stressed out, the stress response we're most aligned with will take over – even if it's totally inappropriate and over the top. The easiest way to really understand this is if I try to fill out the theory with some real life stories.

---

[1] Sometimes, a person can also be experiencing inherited trauma, too. (That topic is outside the scope of this book, but if you'd like to explore it further on your own, take a look at the RESOURCES section at the back of the book.)

TEARING INTO CLIENTS

Alice the book editor is a Type 4 personality, a Motivator-Builder. When Alice isn't operating from a place of stress, she can speak her mind in a friendly, upbeat and helpful way that really helps squeeze the best work out of her clientele.

But when Alice gets stressed, her friendly directness can start to morph into some pretty harsh, personal criticism of her authors. Instead of enthusiastic motivation, Alice starts tearing her clients to pieces (FIGHT) – and that's really bad for business. Over the years, Alice has lost out many times by taking her stress-induced anger out on her clients, who then decided they didn't want to work with her anymore.

If Alice could start to recognize how an over the top stress response is hijacking her useful Motivator-Builder character and causing her to pick pointless fights with her clients (and a bunch of other people in her life, too), think how that could start to transform her interactions, career prospects and bank account!

Let's take another example.

Arnie, a very capable and popular commercial lawyer, is a Builder-Connector. When he's not stressed, he can explain complicated legal jargon in very simple terms to his clients, and also advise them in a very down-to-earth, practical and friendly way.

Arnie got a new secretary who was a pretty unfriendly, unbalanced Builder-Motivator. She was very capable and organized, but also extremely controlling and fairly bristling with passive-aggression. Whenever Arnie asked her to do something for him, he got the impression he was annoying her.

Over time, Arnie started to feel more and more stressed around his secretary which manifested itself in Arnie trying to avoid having anything to do with her. Arnie tried to get to the office before she showed up for the day so he could get behind his desk without having to make small talk with her. And when he did have to ask her to do something for him – which after all, was actually the woman's job – Arnie approached his secretary apologetically, as though he was asking her for a favor.

Over time, Arnie felt increasingly miserable in his job, but felt he couldn't tackle his secretary head on and explain what the problem was (FLATTER). Arnie felt it was easier to look for a new job (FLIGHT), than to risk a potentially unpleasant confrontation with his subordinate.

If Arnie had realized his stress response had taken over, which is why he felt like running away, it would have been a big step forward on the road to developing a more balanced and helpful response to dealing with the source of his stress, i.e. his difficult secretary.

Again, the stress response isn't bad, *per se*, but it has to be applied judiciously and appropriately. It stands to reason that if we're experiencing a lot of stress in our lives we will be operating out of that 'stressed' place far more often than not, and doing so usually has some big consequences that arise based on how we managed our difficulties, came through our challenges, and handled our relationships.

For example, if Arnie could apply a little more FIGHT to the unbalanced relationship dynamic he has with his secretary and start to stand up for himself a little more, it would go a long way toward solving the problem. While you might believe anger is always 'bad', the People Smarts System doesn't hold by that.

Sometimes, we need that anger and aggression to stand up for ourselves, and to stop other people from taking advantage of us. If don't have some steel in our characters, if we don't have some backbone, how are we going to protect ourselves and protect other vulnerable people in society?

When we're using our anger in this way, it's actually a positive trait. But as soon as that anger and aggression becomes self-serving, or bullying, or domineering, then it's out of balance and it's destroying the world instead of building it.

When we're in balance, we can choose which of the four main stress responses of FIGHT-FLIGHT-FREEZE-FLATTER might be the most appropriate to help us deal with a stressful situation, interaction or relationship. But in the meantime, most of us will have one or two main responses to stress that typically show up whenever the pressure starts to pile on.

NO ONE SIZE FITS ALL

A big difference between modern psychology and the *People Smarts* System is that where psychology takes a blanket approach to personality and makes generalizations about particular traits being negative or positive, the *People Smarts* System provides a typology that enables each person to identify what traits and characteristics are innately theirs, and how to bring out the positive side of that trait instead of trying to totally eradicate it.

There are no 'broken brains' or labels in the *People Smarts* System. Rather, the focus is on getting an out-of-control stress response to calm down, so that the true beauty of the personality that's underneath can come shining through.

The last thing to underline before we take a closer look at each of the stress responses is that there is so much more to our personality than just our stress response. Once we start to identify and reduce our internal and external sources of stress, our energy can be freed up, and new abilities can crystallize as a result that can help us in so many ways.

For example, the exact same energy that powers an angry response can be transformed into a determination to keep persevering, even when everyone else gave up a long time ago. That's a very valuable skill to have. Later on in the book we'll explore in much more detail how we can take the raw energy contained in these stress responses and use it to open doors and start to tap into and develop our true potential.

Now that we've explained what the stress response is, and how it gets triggered, in the next chapter we'll take a deep-dive into how the four different stress responses actually look in real time.

IDENTIFIYING YOUR MAIN STRESS RESPONSE

If our life is very stressful – if we're dealing with a severe shortage of cash, a serious health problem, a difficult relationship or three, if someone we love just died, if something we care about is really not happening, or coming together, or maybe even if it's falling apart, if we're spending eight hours a day in a job or situation we hate - we're going to feel pretty stressed.

Recognizing how overwhelming stress can 'warp' our personalities and cause us to react in ways that are often unhelpful is a crucial component of the PEOPLE SMARTS SYSTEM. Before we continue, let's just remind ourselves of which personality building block is connected to which stress response.

Under stress:

MOTIVATION can devolve into **FIGHT,** often characterized by anger, rage, hatred, jealousy, aggression and stubbornness.

CONNECTION can devolve into **FLIGHT**, often characterized by anxiety, worry, fear, obsessive-compulsion and an urge to run away from the problem.

PHILOSOPHICAL THINKING can devolve into **FREEZE,** often characterized by sadness and depression, self-isolation, heaviness, despair and apathy.

BUILDING can devolve into **FLATTER**, often characterized by people-pleasing, losing the self, superficiality, and an inability to stand up for ourselves.

Sometimes, even the negative characteristics described here are a VERY appropriate way of acting and reacting to dangerous people and situations. If you are in a dangerous environment, situation or relationship, your stress response will be pinging off way more than if you're sunning yourself by the beach in the Bahamas – *and that's actually the way it's meant to be.*

The real issues only start to show up when our reaction to stress is *inappropriate*. What does that mean, in practice? An *inappropriate* reaction to stress is when we find ourselves **over**-reacting to our circumstances or feeling 'stressed' by things that are objectively no big deal, and then *whoosh!!* Before we even know what's happening, the stress response has taken over and we've lost control of ourselves.

This happens to all of us from time to time, particularly if we happen to be going through a lot of difficulties and challenges, but if that's happening a lot more than you'd like, or if it's starting to interfere with your relationships, career or life goals, then be aware that you probably need to take a sober look at your circumstances and relationships to see how you can change things up so that you aren't being constantly triggered into an inappropriate reaction.

So, overreacting to objectively small issues and problems is one big sign that you're stressed. Another key thing to look at when you're trying to identity an *inappropriate* reaction is when you keep getting stuck in one particular mode or response that doesn't actually fit the circumstances you're in.

DON'T WALK ON THE GRASS

Before I started writing this book I took a short holiday with my family up North to spend some time swimming in lakes and relaxing in nature. Apart from my teenagers' awful taste in music, we actually all got on pretty well for the first couple of days.

But then I made the mistake of taking them out to a local strip mall to get ice-cream. It was a baking hot, sultry afternoon, and it was hard to find parking. Once I'd parked the car and got the ice-cream, we all realized that the only free seats were stuck in an unshaded area getting totally blasted by the sun.

One of my kids decided to sit under the shade of a tree in the fenced-off grassy area, and after umming and ahhing for a bit, I decided to join her. At this point I was already starting to feel pretty stressed and irritated. I'm a Philosopher-Motivator, so my 'idealist' was already a little disappointed with whoever designed the seating arrangements, and my motivator was getting a bit frustrated at how the afternoon was turning out.

But hey! Mint choc chip can lift anyone's mood! So I was sitting there under the tree, stuffing the ice-cream into my face when one of the Mall workers drove past, stopped, and started yelling at me for sitting under the tree in the fenced-off area.

Initially, the Motivator side flared into FIGHT – but this guy wasn't about to back down, and he really went to town on how inappropriate I was behaving, sitting and eating ice-cream under that tree where people weren't meant to be, when there were seats all over the place.

At some point I realized this guy was just going to keep yelling at me for as long as he wanted to and there was nothing I could to shut him up, which is when I got hit by a really strong FREEZE reaction that instantly turned me into a depressed-feeling zombie. I didn't want to be around my kids or my husband. I didn't want to be on holiday any more eating ice-cream. I just wanted to go somewhere and cry.

Was this a reasonable, rational response to being told to keep of the grass? Not really. Sure, the guy was acting like a jerk, but going into FREEZE at that point wasn't helping to resolve the situation, and it seriously threatened to spoil the whole holiday. A better reaction would have been to walk away (FLIGHT), or to apologize and try to appease him (FLATTER), or if he was being really abusive, to up the ante and start loudly threatening to sue him (FIGHT).

But FREEZE wasn't helping anyone.

So, that's what I mean about getting 'stuck' in a stress response that's not really taking you where you need to go. Nor does it resolve the problem. Often, it just makes the situation worse.

Before you really learn about the four stress responses of FIGHT, FLIGHT, FREEZE and FLATTER, and understand how all these 'Four Fs' can literally hi-jack our brains and cause us to act and react in ways that we really don't like or want, it's very easy to think that this is just how it is and there is nothing you can really do about it.

So before we dive into the descriptions, I want to point out, nice and clearly, that you shouldn't let all this stuff get you down or stress you out when you start to read it. Some of it's not so nice, some of it's a bit ugly, it's true, but with a bit of knowledge and effort, all of these characteristics can be transformed into something very positive.

If you take just one thing away from this book, let it be this:

We are not our stress response.

Our stress response is a component of our character and it contains a lot of raw power and energy, but it's not **the real us.** Later on, I'll discuss some proven hacks you can use to identify what's stressing you out, and how you can begin to ratchet down your stress level. But in the meantime, let's take a look at each of the four stress responses in turn.

As you read through the descriptions, try to catch how you typically react when you start feeling stressed. If you're having difficulties identifying which stress response is dominant, try asking a friend or family member for some input or refer back to the response you got from the *People Smarts 16 Personality* System Quiz.

(You can also take the quiz online at http://peoplesmartsbook.com/quiz and encourage family members and friends to take the quiz, too, to start getting more solid answers about what's really happening, and why.)

THE FIGHT RESPONSE:

Is typically characterized by:

- 'Self-preservation' at all costs
- Explosive temper and outbursts
- Aggressive, angry behavior
- A pronounced need to control (both people and situations)
- Bullying
- Domineering and controlling behavior
- Inability to 'hear' or accept other points of view
- A pronounced sense of entitlement

- Demands for other people to be 'perfect'
- Dictatorial tendencies

The **FIGHT** response is usually the dominant stress reaction of **MOTIVATOR** personality types.

THE FLIGHT RESPONSE:

Is typically characterized by:

- Obsessive and / or compulsive behavior
- Feelings of panic and anxiety
- Rushing around
- Over-worrying
- Workaholic
- Paranoid thoughts
- Can't sit still, can't relax
- Micromanaging situations and other people
- Always 'on the go', busy doing things
- Wants things to be perfect
- Overachiever

The **FLIGHT** response is usually the dominant stress reaction of **CONNECTOR** personality types.

THE FREEZE RESPONSE:

Is typically characterized by:

- Spacing out
- Feeling unreal
- Hibernating
- Isolating the self from the outside world

- Couch potato
- Disassociating
- Brain fog
- Feeling disconnected
- Difficulty in making decisions, acting on decisions
- Achievement-phobic
- Wants to hide from the world
- Feeling 'dead', lifeless

The **FREEZE** response is usually the dominant stress reaction of **PHILOSOPHER** personality types.

THE FLATTER RESPONSE:

Is typically characterized by:

- People pleasing
- Scared to have their own opinion and say what they really think
- Wants to talk about 'the other' instead of themselves
- Flatters others (to avoid conflict)
- 'Angel of mercy'
- Over-cares, takes too much responsibility for others
- Acts like a 'sucker'
- Prefers superficial interactions and relationships
- Can't stand up for the self, can't say 'no'
- Easily exploited by others
- Hugely concerned with social standing and acceptance, 'fitting in'
- 'Yes' man (or woman…)
- Passive aggression

The **FLATTER** response is usually the dominant stress reaction of **BUILDER** personality types.

THE 'STRESS' PERSONALITY

Remember, when we start acting in some of the ways described above, that's not the real us. It's just a function of our personality under stress.

The key to good emotional health, and by extension developing happy, loving and long-lasting relationships, is to work on ensuring this 'stress personality' of ours only comes out when it's needed, and is not in the driving seat.

We're not talking about totally negating parts of our character here, or labeling all negative emotions as 'bad' or 'wrong'. There is a time and a place for anger, for running away, for disconnecting, and for placating other people. These reactions are often helpful and healthy.

But often, they are not.

And that's where we need to focus our attention now, to see how we can transform the underlying energy and potential contained in an 'inappropriate' stress response into something that's truly useful and positive both for ourselves, and the people around us.

So how do we actually do that? Read on!

THE BASIC PRINCIPLES OF ACHIEVING BALANCE

Everything in this world has its own job to do. The sun's job is to heat our world sufficiently to enable life to flourish, without burning us to a crisp. The atmosphere has a job is to provide us with just enough of the oxygen we need to breathe, and to maintain our environment. The clouds' job is to give us enough rain to water our plants and let us have the CO_2 we need to drink. Meanwhile, it's the earth's job to provide us with a foundation to build on, and a mechanism for growing the food that will sustain us.

When the earth is balanced and operating in harmony, we have enough warmth; the rain appears during the right season and in the right amounts; we have clean air to breathe and fertile ground to develop.

Balance doesn't mean trying to turn dust into heat, or water into oxygen. Balance means that each element is functioning correctly, doing its own job in the world in the most optimal and beneficial way. And the same is also true of us, and our personalities.

Getting balanced doesn't mean trying to turn a passionate and extroverted MOTIVATOR type into something they're really not. It just means ensuring that the MOTIVATOR'S passion is being channeled outwards appropriately, so instead of burning bridges and destroying relationships, it's being used to light up a room and inspire warm, loving feelings between people.

The goal of the People Smarts System is to enable us to bring out the positive side of our Personality Type and to minimize the negative side. When we're balanced, we can temper our main, stress-response induced approach to life with some of the skill sets and abilities that are generally found within another personality building block.

OPENING NEW DOORS WITH A BALANCED APPROACH

As I mentioned earlier, I'm a Philosopher-Motivator – a slightly crazy mix of PHILOSOPHICAL THINKING's idealism and emotional intensity stirred together with MOTIVATION's passionate energy and enthusiasm. Until I figured out the People Smarts System, I'd written more than 10 self-help books and barely sold a handful of copies. Why? Because I was struggling to bring all my ideas and insights down to earth and discover how to share them with my readers in a way they could understand and apply in a manner that would really help them in their lives.

To put this into *People Smarts* language, I was lacking some of the CONNECTORS' easy communication and ability to lighten things up, and also some of the BUILDERS' ability to sugar-coat things and make them more palatable and acceptable to other people. Once I realized that, it helped me come up with a completely different way of framing the *People Smarts System*.

Instead of trying to hit people over the head with the information (MOTIVATOR), and to blast them into pieces with some over the top, idealistic, ultimately unpalatable home truths (PHILOSOPHICAL THINKING), I started focusing on trying to bring more of the points out via personal stories (CONNECTION), and to focus way more on the positive than on the negative (BUILDING).

Once I understood that I needed to adopt a more balanced approach to putting all this stuff out there, the *People Smarts System* was born and this book finally got written.

INNER BALANCE VS. OUTER BALANCE

So, one way getting more balanced can definitely help us is by enabling us to figure out the best *Personality Smarts* way to approach our projects, careers, and other goals and dreams, and to understand how to smooth off some of the rough edges in our personalities and attitudes that might be tripping us up and holding us back.

When we're really at peace inside and we feel like we're doing what we're meant to be doing in the way we're meant to be doing it, and we also start to like and appreciate ourselves way more, I call that being in a place of 'Inner Balance'.

Until we've figured out how to get more 'Inner Balance', we're going to struggle mightily to get the second half of the equation sorted out, which I call 'Outer Balance'. 'Outer Balance' refers to our relationships, and how we interact with other people on the planet. Because when all the different personalities can start to appreciate the aptitudes and abilities of other people and start to harness the power of different personalities working together, that's when really amazing things start to happen in the world.

To put this a different way, Outer Balance is when the 16 different personality types can synthesize their different talents and outlooks to start building positive, and even radical, changes in the world. But again, let me underline that this type of Outer Balance can only start to happen when there is true Inner Balance between the four personality building blocks within the individual.

It's probably obvious why that's the case, but let's set it out nice and clearly before we move on to discussing how we can actually start moving into that place of Inner Balance. If we're constantly reacting and overreacting from an unbalanced, unreasonable and stressed place, that can make it pretty hard for us to get along with other people and to sustain lasting, loving and responsible relationships. The more we can operate out of that place of Inner Balance, where stress-induced overreactions are kept to a bare minimum, the happier we'll feel, and the easier we'll find it to love, and be loved.

MANDY THE MOTHER-IN-LAW

As a Builder-Motivator, Mandy's home life was very important to her. She married young, and immediately went about the job of creating 'the perfect family home'. Mandy's husband and kids quickly learned that expressing negative emotions publically upset Mandy a lot, so the family fell into the habit of interacting with each other in a casual, superficial way where deep feelings and different ideas were left unsaid.

This worked fairly well until Mandy's children grew up and started bringing their partners home. The first time Mandy's daughter Lisa brought Ian home to meet her, he thought she was sweet if a little bossy. Mandy was a good talker and very personable, so Ian initially felt very comfortable around her.

But as time went on, Ian, increasingly started to chafe at Mandy's unspoken expectations that he and Lisa, Mandy's daughter, should come over and visit her every weekend. Lisa found herself caught between Ian and her mother's competing expectations, and started to feel overwhelmed and torn between them.

Ian was a Connector-Motivator, which meant that while he usually preferred to work around awkward situations, he wasn't scared to stand up for himself when the situation demanded it. Lisa, a Philosopher-Builder, could see where a confrontation between Ian and Mandy would lead, and was very unhappy about the situation. But she felt paralyzed, and unable to step in and resolve things.

After applying the *People Smarts* principles of Inner Balance to the issue, Lisa came to understand that she actually had a crucial role to play in moving Ian and Mandy past their FIGHT-fueled face-off. But first, she had to summon up some of her own inner Motivator to give her the strength to broach the topic, and also the ability to put some reasonable, but firm boundaries in place.

MOTIVATION knows what it wants, and where it's going, so Lisa had to take some time to stop reacting to other people's demands and to figure out how much she herself actually wanted to see Mandy, and under what circumstances. Once she took the time to dig a little deeper into her own real feelings about what was going on, Lisa was surprised to discover that she was actually far closer to Ian's position than she'd realized.

As a Philosopher-Builder, Lisa was able to avoid a flare-up with Mandy by gently moving to less frequent visits, and also arranging to see her mother for coffee breaks at the mall without Ian. This reassured Mandy that she was still an important part of Lisa's life, and avoided triggering Mandy into trying to force Lisa to pick her side over Ian's. As Ian started to feel less controlled by Mandy and her unreasonable expectations, his more easy-going CONNECTOR side resurfaced and he started to get along with Mandy much better on the rare occasions they actually saw each other. Ian also stopped feeling so much resentment at Lisa for putting so much effort into her mother, at what he felt was his expense.

The key to achieving more Outer Balance in Lisa's relationships depended on her first getting more Inner Balance, so she could stand up for herself and take a more active role in guiding the relationship with Mandy.

THE PRINCIPLES OF INNER AND OUTER BALANCE

So, what does it actually *mean* to be 'balanced', internally?

While that's a subject that you could probably write a whole encyclopedia about, and still not cover all the bases, the following principles sum it up. When we're operating from a place of Inner Balance it means we can easily move between:

- Doing and being
- Having the determination to carry on and knowing when it's time to let go
- Feeling wired, motivated and tense and feeling relaxed, calm and peaceful
- Paying attention to detail and seeing the bigger picture
- Intensely focusing on the present and being able to learn from the past, and daydreaming about the future

Outer Balance applies to how we interact with others. When we're operating from a place of Outer Balance that means we can easily move between:

- Asserting ourselves and giving way to others
- Putting something out and receiving something back
- Talking to others and listening to others
- Helping other people and accepting help ourselves

- Taking the lead and letting others go first and set the direction
- Standing up for what's right and making peace with others

All of these things, and more, are required for each of us to get to a place of true 'balance', and each of us will begin that journey from a different point on the scale. For example, while a PHILOSOPHER personality will usually find it much easier to see the bigger picture, they'll often have much more of a struggle finding enough motivation and applying enough attention to detail to take concrete steps forward towards their goals or dreams.

And while a BUILDER personality like Lisa will normally have no problem smoothing things over and making up with people, standing up for what's right can often be a massive stretch out of their comfort zone.

Yet achieving this balance between the different traits that make up the four personality building blocks is the key to achieving true *People Smarts*, which means we understand why we act and react the way we do, how we interact with others – and what areas we need to work on and balance out to start living the best life we could possibly have.

This is the main job we're down here to do, and I'll tell you straight that it's not a quick fix. It can honestly take a lifetime for us to get to that place of true inner and out balance, but every step in the right direction will bring us enormous rewards in the here and now.

FINDING THE GOLDEN MEAN

So, we've got to the question of questions: **how do we start to get more balanced?**

I will go into way more detail over the following chapters, but the basic rule of thumb is that each person needs to find the 'golden mean' between the personality traits they already have, and the ones they need to work to acquire.

It shakes down like this:

MOTIVATION and BUILDING are at opposite ends of one personality continuum and CONNECTION and PHILOSOPHICAL THINKING are at opposite ends of the other.

The more of the traits of **MOTIVATION** you have in your personality, the more you will need to acquire the traits associated with **BUILDING**, and vice-versa.

And the more **CONNECTION** traits you naturally have, the more you'll need to work to acquire the traits associated with **BUILDING** – and again, vice-versa.

It's important to stress that **we're not talking about trying to change ourselves into something we're not**. When I talk about getting balanced, what that really means is developing the ability to choose a different mode of behaving or reacting when we're under stress that may not come naturally, but that will help us to reach the internal goals or the relationship outcomes we actually want.

A big part of being able to do this properly is simply to recognize what our starting point is by understanding what our basic personality might be. Once a PHILOSOPHER personality type starts to acknowledge that they have a tendency to be drawn towards unrealistic idealism and inertia, for example, they can identify where their strong PHILOSOPHICAL THINKING and FREEZE reaction might need balancing out with the lightness and agility of CONNECTION, for example.

Or perhaps the PHILOSOPHER personality needs a little more of MOTIVATION's determination and energy, or more of BUILDING's forgiving and accepting nature. The idea is not to totally dismantle our innate personality. Rather, to simply move away from being stuck in a 'default' mode that is often not so helpful, and to choose a much more balanced and selective approach to life, as the following story shows.

UNDER THE THUMB

Jon was a Type 12 personality, a Philosopher-Builder. He had a well-paying job in finance, a good marriage, two nice kids, and thanks to his wealthy father-in-law, a spacious house in a good neighborhood.

But increasingly, Jon was miserable. Richard, his father-in-law was a Motivator-Builder – he had a very charming and friendly side, but was also a control freak who used his cash to manipulate his family into doing exactly what he wanted. Richard had a key to Jon's house, and he'd let himself in whenever he felt like it – regardless of whether it was convenient for Jon and his wife.

As a Type 13 Pure Builder, Jon's wife found it impossible to stand up to her father. She did her best to maintain a superficial peace between her husband and her father that didn't look too closely at the toll Richard's unreasonable demands were starting to take on her family life.

Jon usually responded to Richard's control-freakery by trying to play it down and making an effort to see the good in his father-in-law. But as time went on, he found himself feeling more and more like the guest at his own table. His deeper Philosopher side was too honest and insightful to keep pretending everything was fine, so Jon started to feel more and more depressed and 'stuck'.

Things came to a head during their vacation. Ever summer Richard insisted that Jon, Sally and the kids fly out to a destination that he chose and paid for – but which left them effectively as Richard's prisoners for two weeks, unable even to take a day off to do their own thing or choose their own schedule.

Jon had recently celebrated his 40th birthday, and all the dissatisfaction, boredom and frustration he'd been pushing down for years started gushing out. Shortly beforehand, he'd been overlooked for another promotion at work with his boss telling him they were looking for someone with greater leadership potential and flair. Jon had been in the same job for years and the pay was good, but he was scared to branch out and try something different. More and more it seemed like his job was a dead-end.

Richard typically booked a minivan on vacation that would take his extended family to wherever Richard had decided they should go that day. That morning they were supposed to go see a local waterfall that was a two hour drive away, when some of Jon's missing MOTIVATION finally started to reassert itself.

With a start, he realized he didn't want to go to the waterfall - and that he was sick of being treated like a kid by Richard. As Jon's missing MOTIVATION started to resurface, he realized he wanted to find a different job and to move to a different area far away from Richard's interference.

It took Jon well over a year to finally put these plans into action, but being able to access his missing MOTIVATION and CONNECTION enabled him to move out of his depressed, comfortable rut and to take back control of his life.

One of the best things about the *People Smarts System* is that it really doesn't require a lot of effort for things to start moving in a very positive direction. Even just starting to notice how your stress response may be shaping your reactions and interactions, and starting to make a little space to think about how things could change, is enough to get the ball rolling. Even if all you do is read this book, you will already have planted a very powerful seed in your mind for the new, more balanced, approach to life you want to take.

So now it's time to take this discussion out of the realm of theory, and to show you how to start applying the *People Smarts System* to getting balanced in real time.

THE 5 PEOPLE SMARTS PRINCIPLES OF BALANCE

Before we get into a detailed discussion of what the different personality types will need to focus on specifically, I first want to set down the 5 *People Smarts* Principles of Balance that apply across all 16 *People Smarts* personality types.

Each personality type will have a different way of relating to each of these principles, and I'll give more details of what to watch out for, specifically, when we get into the discussion about how to balance each of the 4 personality building blocks a little later on.

The more we work on incorporating these ideas into our approach to life, the easier we'll find it to stop falling into a stress-induced, default 'extreme' response, that's often just causing us a lot of emotional difficulties and relationship problems.

PEOPLE SMARTS BALANCE PRINCIPLE 1: AVOID PERFECTIONISM

If life was 'perfect', then we wouldn't have to deal with difficult or overwhelming emotions, or with massive disappointments, let downs, challenges and heartbreaks. But the world isn't perfect, and it never will be.

Working on accepting this very basic fact of life can go a long ways toward reducing the ferocity of an Elemental overreaction, and can help us have a much more balanced view of what areas of our life could use some work.

The world is a very imperfect place, and we are a very imperfect part of it. That doesn't mean that we stop trying, or that we stop making our best efforts, but it does mean that we stop having unreasonable expectations of ourselves and other people, and start to accept our limitations.

Aiming for 'perfect' usually just makes us very stressed, and when we're stressed, it's far harder to choose against our default Four Element response – even if it's not so helpful!

Focusing on the following things can help us start to defuse our 'perfectionistic' tendencies:

- Focusing on the good, instead of trying to seek out the bad
- Easing up on other people, and also on ourselves, when we don't manage to be 'perfect'
- Aiming for 'good enough', instead of 100% perfect
- Setting realistic expectations and going one baby step at a time towards achieving them

PEOPLE SMARTS BALANCE PRINCIPLE 2: MINIMIZE THE PROBLEM, (AKA ADOPT THE 'NO BIG DEAL' APPROACH TO LIFE)

Newspaper editors learned a very long time ago that headlines proclaiming the end of the world routinely got far more people buying papers than headlines saying: *Everything is doing pretty good, nothing to worry about here.*

Sure, there *is* a lot of crazy stuff happening all the time and we all have our fair share of dramatic developments to deal with. But the human brain simply wasn't built to handle non-stop crises and bad news.

With the rise of social media many of us have learned to frame our own crises and challenges in the most bombastic and hysterical terms possible in order to stand out from the crowd and get some attention. Instead of going that far, or ignoring our problems by pretending everything is A-OK when it isn't, we should take a few seconds to think about whether the difficult situation we're in, or the massive problem we're having, is really as bad as it looks before we slam the panic button.

In the heat of the moment, especially at the beginning of this process, that will be pretty hard to do. So initially, we just need to notice our reaction. Then, over the next days when the 'drama' has dissipated a little, we can go back into whatever just happened and start to explore some of the assumptions we made when we were operating from a place of feeling stressed-out.

The key is just to devote some time to thinking about the subject and to start asking a few pertinent questions about what really happened, like:

- Did the reaction really 'fit' the situation?
- Did I over-react, under-react or run away?

- If I could do it all over again, would I change how I reacted?
- What would I try to do differently? Why?
- What were the consequences of me reacting the way I did?
- Am I pleased with those results? Why or why not?
- How would I feel if someone had reacted that way to me?

Maybe you'll toss these questions around in your mind while you go for a walk or do some T'ai Chi, or while you sit on your deck sipping coffee and watching the sun go down. Maybe, you'll be able to start thinking things through while you wash the dishes or clean the car. Maybe, you'll need a bit more help.

Maybe you'll need some sort of prop to help you, like mind-mapping what just happened, or typing it up as a short story on your computer, or dictating it into your phone like a reporter filing a story at the scene of a crime.

Most of the time, we totally overreact to all the petty issues and mundane difficulties and disappointments that everyone's life is full of. Setting the intention to deliberately play things down will save a lot of wear and tear on our bodies and minds and give us the ability to thinks things through much more clearly without getting tripped into panic, rage or overwhelm.

If you decide you need a stronger response, you can always deliver it in a far more calm and helpful way later on.

Each time we take the time to explore our reactions in this way, and try to play things down instead of playing things up, we are training our brains to become much less reactive to 'bad news', little shocks and disappointments. And over time, we'll find it far easier to choose a more suitable Four Elements response to life's little dramas without just automatically getting sucked into a default option that really may not be helpful.

FAILING THE TEST

Ten year old Ellis tried to slide through the door before his mother would notice but, poor kid, she'd been waiting for him to show up for half an hour already and at the first creak of the latch Mary shot out of the kitchen to ask the question Ellis was dreading:

"How'd it go?"

She was referring to the math test that was meant to determine if Ellis was a 'gifted' child or not, and whether or not he'd be eligible for a scholarship to the private school upstate next year. Ellis gulped.

"Not so well," he croaked out. Mary stared at him, horrified. Mary, an unbalanced Motivator-Connector, couldn't believe her ears.

"How could you do that to me, Ellis?" she admonished him, as he stood there wishing the floor would open up and swallow him. Ellis felt so miserable that he couldn't even raise his eyes to look at his mother. He knew how much she'd been hoping he'd ace this test, and what a big difference Mary felt it would make to his future to pass.

"I'm going to phone the school and demand an explanation," Mary said, pulling out her mobile with a furious look on her face. Ellis cringed. "That teacher of yours has been coasting all year and now we're paying the price!" He hated it when his mother went on the war path and started throwing her weight around and criticizing people. In the middle of all this Dan, Ellis's dad, called home to see how the test went.

"Pretty bad," Ellis whispered into the phone. Dan, a successful lawyer, was a Connector-Builder. He wasn't as passionate or volatile as Mary, but he was still extremely upset by his son's news. "Now Ellis, this is what happens when we spend too much time on our phones, and not enough time on our homework," he began. "We get repaid for our effort, and it seems that not enough effort was put into this, son."

Dan was a perfectionistic, and he simply couldn't understand how his son hadn't spent hours burning the candle at both ends during his studies, practicing the exercises over and over again, the way he himself would have.

Mary got hold of Mr. Angel, the math teacher, a Builder-Philosopher personality type, and was blasting him for his alleged laziness and easy going attitude with the class. Mr. Angel was apologizing profusely, and doing anything he could to calm her down and defuse the situation. After he hung up, he went into the teacher's lounge and sat down on one of the chairs as a sense of crushing guilt started to descend upon him. Maybe Mary was right. Maybe his easy-going attitude had ruined Ellis's chances of doing well on the test, and spoiled his chance of getting into the better school. Mr. Angel started to feel pretty down.

All of this drama, all of this upset - and what actually happened?

Nothing much. A kid got a bad mark on a test. Can you imagine how different all these mundane challenges would look and feel if, instead of playing it up and getting hysterical, all of us made more of an effort to play these things down, instead?

PEOPLE SMARTS BALANCE PRINCIPLE 3: VALIDATE AND ACCEPT OUR OWN EXPERIENCES AND FEELINGS

A few problems can occur when we don't properly identify, describe or connect to our real feelings:

- The 'lost' feelings can wreak havoc in our physical and emotional system, leading to all sorts of psychosomatic issues.

- The energy from that feeling doesn't disappear. Usually, it'll get transformed into the emotion that describes our dominant Four Elemental Stress Response.

- We can feel very lonely and disconnected from others, even the people we are closest to. If we can't tell others what we're really experiencing and feeling about things, it can lead to superficial and unsatisfying relationships, and a mounting sense of internal anxiety.

- We don't feel comfortable in our own skin, or head-space. The lost feelings are always trying to remind us they're still there and need to be acknowledged, and that can be one of the most unpleasant, uncomfortable feelings in the world.

- We have no idea what message our feelings are trying to give us about what needs to change in our life in order for us to feel happier and more content.

A WORD ON PROJECTION

Sometimes, when our brain gives us the message that's it's too dangerous for us to honestly accept and acknowledge our true feelings and thoughts about things, or it's too upsetting for us to honestly acknowledge certain parts of our personality that we don't like very much, we can end up projecting this stuff onto other people – usually without even realizing it.

Trying to identify our true feelings about things, and making the connections between our moods and experiences is a core skill that many of us were never taught, but which needs to be worked on regularly if we want to achieve some real Elemental Balance.

We should try to regularly take our 'emotional pulse' to avoid getting blindsided by an unhelpful or over-reactive stress response that we didn't see coming, because we don't know what feeling is really hiding out underneath the anger, anxiety, space-out or fake nice.

Making these links between potential stressors and our subsequent moods can help us to develop:

- Healthy boundaries
- Healthy self-awareness
- More ability to avoid / defuse / challenge stressful situations from the outset, before they take us out emotionally.

Once we have a better idea what we really think and feel about a whole bunch of the people and situations in our life, we'll find that our stress response calms down and a lot of the irritation, overwhelm and anxiety will be replaced over time with a tolerance for others that's born of a much deeper understanding of how 'life' is affecting us – and how we might be affecting others, for both good and bad.

PEOPLE SMARTS BALANCE PRINCIPLE 4: STOP TRYING TO CONTROL OTHER PEOPLE

When we get scared, or feel anxious, or start to feel threatened in some way, we usually try to reassure ourselves about what's happening by pulling back and trying to regain control of the situation. Depending on our personality type, we'll try to do this in different ways.

MOTIVATOR personalities often use anger and criticism to try to regain control of a relationship; CONNECTORS often resort to using hard-work, micro-management and a sense of humor to get back into a place of feeling as though they can control the outcome; PHILOSOPHERS try to take back control by taking themselves out of the situation and retreating; while BUILDERS often try to control by swiftly papering over any cracks that are appearing and maintaining a stoic attitude of 'business as usual'.

Sometimes, depending on the situation, this can be a helpful response. But the trouble is that really, there is far less in our control than we'd like to think. Accepting that ultimately we are not in control and that we can't really solve our problems by controlling other people and other people's reactions, is a key principle of achieving Elemental Balance.

Often, so much of the friction we experience in our relationships is either because someone is trying to control us, or we're trying to control someone else. Controlling behavior rarely comes from a place of balance, which is why understanding who is controlling and who is being controlled is a really good place to start in the quest for balance – particularly Outer Balance.

Life is constantly trying to teach us new things and encourage us to widen our ability to think and develop new skills. When we stay in our comfort zones, all these latent abilities stay hidden and undeveloped – and we never reach our full potential. But when we're willing to let go of what we want and how we think it should be done, at least a little, and when we're willing to endure a little emotional discomfort, we can reap some enormous rewards.

Let's try to put this another way. When we get stuck in old, rigid patterns of thinking and reacting to things, we end up trying to control more and more of our environment to prevent too much 'change' from seeping through and disturbing our internal equilibrium.

Predictability is safe. Boring doesn't cause overwhelm. But life doesn't always let us control it! And trying to stay on top of everything and everyone is totally exhausting and innately stressful, and is often a big obstacle to achieving elemental balance, particularly in our relationships.

The reasons for this are perhaps obvious. A forceful MOTIVATOR is usually much better at imposing their will on their environment, and the people around them, than the other personality types. But who's to say that the MOTIVATOR'S way of doing things is always correct? Some amazing synergies with others can occur when we start to let go of our compulsion to control, and to do things 'our way'.

CHOOSING HOW WE REACT

What could happen if we *choose* to react to challenges, difficulties and relationship issues in a different way? That's a scary question for a lot of people, but when we start to ask ourselves about what might happen, if we *choose* to see an argument more from the other person's point of view; or what could happen if we *choose* to step off the path of predictability to follow our dreams, the answers can often lead us to a far more satisfying and fulfilling life.

Thinking these thoughts don't oblige us to act on them, they just start to open up more possibilities and make it easier for us to understand that there are many different options and opportunities waiting for us at every point in time.

Life wants to teach us new ways of doing things and to provide us with new and different experiences. We may not like or enjoy all of them, but we will still learn something valuable from every single experience we go through that we can use to build the world in some way.

But only if we start to give way a little more, to move out of our mental rut, and to let go of the reins a little bit.

Every time we work on taking down our control impulse and letting go, we'll find ourselves connecting more to our capacity for evaluating and responding to new information, seeing other people's points of view, and for having a more realistic and optimistic view of where we ourselves are really holding.

And other people really like to be around a person like that, a person who can dream big, tolerate differences of opinion, and who is constantly learning and growing – and encouraging others to do the same.

DOING THINGS DIFFERENTLY

Lucy has been doing things her dad's way for as long as she can remember. When she was in school, her dad, James, made it clear that he wanted her to study languages. A polyglot himself, it was important to Lucy's father, a Motivator-Connector, that his children be cosmopolitan and able to freely converse in a number of different languages.

Lucy, a Builder-Philosopher, was more drawn to biology and the sciences, but out of respect for her father – who'd already threatened to cut her older sister out his will when she started dating someone he didn't approve of – she put her own wishes aside and got her degree in Mandarin Chinese.

As it turned out, Mandarin Chinese speakers became highly sought after when China opened its markets to the West, and Lucy found herself in high demand as a translator. Part of her still regretted the fact that she'd never followed her dream of trying to go to med school, but in the meantime, she enjoyed her work and felt happy that keeping her dad happy had paid off for her.

But James, a self-made millionaire, was becoming increasingly unhappy that Lucy's job was taking her away from home – and out of his orbit - for many long weeks at a time. When Lucy returned from a three week business trip in Beijing, James took her out to supper to welcome her back, and then broke the news to her:

"Darling, I want you to come and work for me in my office."

Lucy looked at him blankly, not quite sure what he was suggesting.

"You don't do any work with China, Dad, why do you need me?"

Thanks to his CONNECTOR side, James could turn on the charm when he had to. Before continuing the conversation, he fumbled in his pocket and brought out a plush, velvet blue jewelry box.

"For you," he said, sliding it gently across the table. Lucy felt confused. She opened the box and found an expensive tennis bracelet inside. "It's beautiful, thanks Dad." Somewhere deep down, Lucy detected a growing sense of discomfort, but she didn't know why. After all, her Dad was being so good to her, so kind.

"Come and work for me, Lucy, I'm getting on and I need someone I can really trust in the office."

Lucy started to feel a little claustrophobic and anxious. "Daddy, I like my job. I learned Chinese for you, remember? It's good that I'm getting to use it." She paused. "And, I'm earning a really good salary."

James had her now. "I'll pay you more," he said evenly. "Whatever you're making, I'll add $10,000." Lucy stared at her father. For a brief moment the PHILOSPHER's tendency to tell the truth flashed up and she understood that she would hate to be his secretary, and she would feel totally suffocated having to be around him every day.

She looked over at James and her stomach sank. She could see he had no intention of accepting 'no' as an answer. Lucy knew from past experience that if she tried to refuse, James would keep upping the ante, alternating between threats and promises until she caved in. That's what had happened when she'd wanted to study medicine, and he'd persuaded her to go into the arts, instead. She sighed a very deep sigh. It was now or never.

She put the bracelet back in the box and slid it gently back towards James.

"Daddy, I can't accept this… I like my job."

She looked at him evenly, waiting for the explosion. James stared back, stunned that she'd refused the bracelet, and also, his request.

"That's final?" he tried again. "Even if your decision upsets me, you won't change your mind? Even if I need you in the office?"

Lucy's unbalanced BUILDER side started clamouring for her to back down, apologize and make peace, but she knew she had to find the MOTIVATION that would enable her to set a healthy boundary with James and stop him from controlling every aspect of her life. She knew there would probably be a big price to pay for going against her father's wishes, but she didn't want to spend the next 30 years living her life only for him.

"It's final," she said softly. "You're a very clever man, Daddy. I'm sure you'll find the right person to help you."

PEOPLE SMARTS BALANCE PRINCIPLE 5: RESPECT BOUNDARIES

The last general 'core skill' to focus on is respecting boundaries – ours and other people's.

Every human being on the planet is a unique mix of the four personality blocks of MOTIVATION, CONNECTION, PHILOSOPHICAL THINKING and BUILDING, and each of us was designed with our own particular skill set and aptitudes. There are things that only we can do, there are insights that only we can have, and innovations that only we can come up with.

But that's only going to happen if we have the time and space and ability to really be the authentic 'us', and to not get lost in 'everybody else's' way of doing things, or thinking, or reacting.

For as long as we feel that other people are crowding our space, asking too much, not really seeing us, or hearing us, or taking us for granted, we can't really act and react the way we'd truly like to.

On the other side of the equation, every time we're crossing the line with other people and using threats, force, guilt trips or manipulation to get them to do what's best for us, instead of what's genuinely best for them, we are also skewing the Outer Balance in some very problematic ways.

So, a key skill is to develop the ability to say 'no' when we need to, and to accept other people's right to say 'no' to us, too.

Respecting boundaries is also a core skill for achieving Inner Elemental Balance. Another term for 'boundaries' in this context is 'self-discipline' – a term which has fallen out of favor in so many ways in our modern times.

Self-discipline can refer to things like getting to bed on time, waking up on time, eating properly and getting enough exercise; but at its most basic, it's the art of *choosing* a course of action instead of simply reacting or giving up.

Every time we count to five before losing our temper, or decide to stick to a commitment we made, or force ourselves to turn off the screen to clean up, or make an effort to explore what we're really thinking and feeling, that's also respecting an internal boundary.

And the more we can set up these internal boundaries and abide by them, the easier we will find it to achieve Inner Balance – and true inner peace and satisfaction.

Now that we've set out the 5 People Smarts Principles of Balance that apply across all 16 personality types, it's time to do a deep dive into each of the four main building blocks of personality, MOTIVATION, CONNECTION, PHILOSOPHICAL THINKING and BUILDING, to see how we can iron-out some of the most damaging and destructive imbalances.

BALANCED MOTIVATION

Moving from anger and 'Me First' to patience and empathy

MOTIVATION'S MAIN STRESS RESPONSE IS: FIGHT

Before we begin, let me remind you of something really important: Motivators rock. Without your courage, leadership, passion and determination, where would the world be? I dread to think…

But the problem comes when Motivators get stuck in an aggressive, 'take no prisoners' mode that can alienate and antagonize other people unnecessarily. This can happen because under stress, healthy MOTIVATION can quickly morph into unhealthy (and even anti-social) FIGHT.

So, in addition to checking on who or what may be triggering your stress in a situation, environment or relationship, and working to reduce it to more manageable levels, here are some of the other traits that MOTIVATORS will need to focus on strengthening in order to achieve balance:

- Empathy and compassion
- Patience
- Forgiveness
- Altruism

Let's go through each of these to define what they are and how they look in practice.

EMPATHY AND COMPASSION

Empathy is the ability to put yourself into another person's shoes and see things from their perspective, while compassion is the ability to feel another person's pain. Neither of these things are really encouraged or applauded in our modern society, where blame, criticism and competition are often the name of the game.

Many MOTIVATORS often feel a strong pull to these things because they can be very powerful motivational tools, at least in the short term. But long term? They just keep upping the ante on our stress, and on everyone else's, too.

That old maxim that you can catch way more flies with honey than vinegar certainly applies here. To put this a different way, MOTIVATORS can have far more of a positive impact on society, and the people around them, too, if they can start to relate to other people's viewpoints and feelings more instead of just trying to bulldoze their way through them.

But when the FIGHT mode is flipped on and **me first** becomes the main focus, it's really, really hard to act with empathy and consideration for other people. Now, here's the thing: when we're already in the middle of a FIGHT, especially at the beginning of this process, it's impossible to effectively turn that around.

I'm telling you that upfront so you keep your expectations realistic and you don't get angry at either me or yourself if you can't immediately get a grip on your rage fits and start acting like Mother Teresa. That's not going to happen.

What *can* happen, however, is that during those times when you aren't actively in FIGHT, you can make a commitment to yourself to spend a few minutes a day going back over any meltdowns or explosions from the previous 24 hours and just consider the other person's experience.

Ask yourself how you would feel if the roles were reversed. What insights can you get from trying to adopt this different perspective on what happened? Does that make you feel less angry? What would you do differently, if you could do it all over again?

If you do this regularly, your ability to empathize will strengthen over time and, increasingly, you'll find it easier to press 'pause' on the rage fit before it totally takes over and sweeps away everything before it. When you're no longer automatically reacting to stressful situations from a place of FIGHT, you'll also be able to spend a few seconds considering your options to see if there is a better way of achieving your ends.

Waiting a few seconds before you blast someone to pieces verbally isn't going to cost you anything. If, after some careful consideration, you decide that FIGHT is still your best option, you can still go for it. But, you may discover that once you learn how to take your stress response off the boil, options like walking away or agreeing to compromise can work far better in terms of defusing a situation or solving a problem.

PATIENCE

Another key area of work for MOTIVATOR personalities is to start trying to build up more patience and tolerance for things not going your way, people not doing what you want them to, and life generally not being perfect and predictable.

Whenever you can, spend a few moments mentally scoping out what 'reasonable expectations' look like so you can avoid the pitfalls of trying to attain perfection. Nothing and nobody is perfect, and that's just the way it is. The more you can internalize this, the more prepared you'll be for the inevitable mess-ups, and the less likely it is that you'll get swept away by an uncontrollable wave of anger when it happens.

It's also helpful for MOTIVATORS to start working on catching some of the harsh judgment calls they often make about other people, or the negative situations they find themselves in. Again, no-one is saying pretend everything is wonderful when it isn't, because I know that is total anathema to MOTIVATORS who want to change things, and fix things, and get it all working better.

But what I'm saying is that in the heat of the moment, it's going to help you way more to play things *down*, and to start bringing your feelings of stress off the boiling point, than to play things *up* and have your head explode in frustration.

Building up tolerance for situations that are not going the way we want them to is some of the hardest inner work a person can do, and that goes double for MOTIVATOR personalities. When FIGHT mode kicks in, the stress chemicals can literally start whizzing around our bodies so fast we physically feel like we're going to explode unless there is some release of the tension.

It's beyond the scope of this book, but energy work and learning how to defuse the FIGHT response at the level of the body can be a real game changer for many MOTIVATOR personalities, especially for those people who are regularly triggered into anger fits that they usually deeply regret once all the stress chemicals have subsided again.

If you can literally feel the tension start to build in your body, you will probably need to do something physical to get it to dissipate if you want to avoid an explosion. You can focus on your breath, you can go pound the pavement, or use energy techniques like the 'Karate Chop' method to start diffusing the tension.

However you choose to tackle it, bear in mind that the FIGHT response is powered by a build-up of stress chemicals, and that you have to find another way of releasing those stress chemicals in a healthy way if you want to develop your ability to avoid automatically lighting up like an Exocet missile.

(In the course that goes along with this book I've got a whole bunch of easy, 'instantly calming' techniques and ideas to share with you.)

The more you can understand what's happening at the physiological level, the more patience you'll start to have for yourself and for others, and the easier you'll be able to tolerate life's inevitable challenges and imperfections.

FORGIVENESS

Walking around with a big list of old grievances and resentments and scores to settle adds a lot of extra stress to our system. Part of what makes MOTIVATORS so effective is that they care, passionately, about many different things, and they often have very strong views about the right and wrong way to do things.

Also, as the old saying goes, *if you want to make an omelet, you have to break some eggs* – and MOTIVATORS often find themselves getting into arguments and treading on other people's toes as part and parcel of their attempts to change the status quo and inspire a different, and hopefully better, way of doing things.

All these things can burden MOTIVATORS with a long list of adversaries and 'enemies' who they have clashed with, fought against, or fallen out with in the past. MOTIVATORS are nobody's fool, and with their strong intuition and fearless approach to life, they aren't scared to take on the difficult people and situations that many other personality types can't deal with.

A lot of those people aren't nice, and can fight dirty. It's understandable that if we've been on the receiving end of some nasty behavior that was never properly apologized for or even acknowledged, the resulting angry feelings can stay with us for a long while afterwards.

But nursing angry feelings and fantasizing about taking revenge against the people who have hurt us only feeds our internal feelings of stress and keeps stoking the flames. Apart from the physical toll this takes on our bodies, keeping ourselves permanently 'stressed' also makes it very hard to avoid flying into an unreasonable, inappropriate or over the top FIGHT reaction when we hit a patch of stress.

I'm not going to belabor the point, but the faster you can forgive people and move on, the better it will be for *you*. Instead of all your energy going into your stress response, you'll free it up to help you come up with more innovative and inspiring ideas to build the world.

Forgiving someone doesn't mean you have to totally forget about the harm they caused you, or the danger they may still pose. Keep your boundaries in place, defend yourself, and stay as far away as you can from dangerous and threatening people – because hanging out with these folk is also a very powerful stressor.

But once we let go of our grudges and our fantasies of paying them back for what they did, we'll free up so much more energy, inspiration and even joy, to plough into projects that will make us so much happier than planning how to pay 'Enemy X' back for being so evil.

As a MOTIVATOR myself, I know this is a hard sell. But that's also why I can tell you from first-hand experience that you can be far more impactful by putting more light out into the world than by tiring yourself out trying to fight all the darkness.

ALTRUISM

The last specific trait that MOTIVATOR personalities need to focus on developing is altruism, which can be defined as doing things for other people without getting any obvious reward or payback.

Again, this mitigates an out-of-control **me first** tendency that can be very pronounced in unbalanced MOTIVATORS, and initially it might seem like a pointless waste of time. If we're not going to get a useful contact, or a helpful piece of information, or a lead, client, advantage or payment from doing something, then why should we waste our time doing it?!?

I hear you!

But practicing altruism will enable us to start to develop some of the idealism, community spirit and depth that are usually the preserve of the PHILOSOPHERS. And a strange thing happens when we start to do nice things for others purely as a no-strings-attached kindness because it's the right thing to do: people start to like us and trust us more.

Getting used to doing quiet kindnesses can make us a whole bunch of friends and go a long way to keeping our relationships intact, healthy and running smoothly. It also starts to teach our brain that if we can push off the urge to win, to destroy the other guy, to score the point, to dominate and impose ourselves on others, while it may seem as though we're losing out in the very short-term, in the long-term, we're really only gaining.

QUICK WINS TO BALANCE MOTIVATION

Try introducing one, some or even all of the following hacks to get more into the 'balanced' mode.

TAKE REGULAR TIMEOUTS

Many Motivators can feel really bad after the event when they couldn't stop themselves from exploding in over-the-top-rage at a loved one, friend or work colleague. Learn to recognize the signs telling you when your stress levels are building to a critical level, and if you feel you're about to explode, remove yourself from the situation or discussion that's making you so tense.

Take a walk around the block, visit the bathroom, 'remember' an appointment or phone call you just have to make – it doesn't matter what. The point is to remove yourself from the stress so the stress chemicals can dissipate and you can take your FIGHT response off the boil.

Use your time away to think about what goal or outcome you'd like to achieve when you return, and what might be the best way of doing that. If you're dealing with someone or something that always presses your buttons, before you put yourself back in the situation, take some time to think through how you can change things up to make the interaction less stressful and tense.

DEALING WITH 'MR. ANGRY' OF THE SKIES

I hate flying, and try to avoid it, but sometimes it's unavoidable. Last summer I had to attend a memorial service for a close relative abroad, and I was dreading it. The flight there was relatively OK, but the flight back was on a budget airline with a psycho head steward named Liam.

Liam was an obviously unbalanced Type 1 personality, Pure Motivator, and he was clearly a very strong personality – but was totally abusing his position and power. It quickly became obvious that the rest of the cabin crew loathed him, and that he intended to rule the flight with an iron fist.

Liam was aggressively forcing passengers back into their seats, arbitrarily closing the toilets and generally acting like an unhinged 'King of the Jungle'. As the flight continued, my stress levels started to spike every time Liam put out yet another ridiculous command over the intercom, "For your comfort and safety, ladies and gentlemen."

Halfway through the flight, Liam went berserk and decided to kick a family with young children off the flight because their baby had developed a temperature of 37.5 degrees. The poor mother had made the mistake of asking Liam for some ibuprofen and now she was about to pay for it. Half an hour later, a hysterical Liam had overruled a doctor and the parents of the child to force the plane to make an unscheduled stop in Bulgaria for 'urgent medical attention'.

I was watching all this unnecessary drama unfold from two rows back, and Liam's ridiculous behavior got me totally stressed. There are few things more stressful for a Philosopher-Motivator like me than being stuck on a plane with a lunatic tin-pot dictator as a Head Steward. But I knew that if I exploded at Liam I'd be the next one turfed out on the tarmac in Bulgaria, as Liam had zero empathy for his passengers and simply couldn't take anyone else's views or opinions into account.

In the meantime, my own FIGHT tendency was starting to build… and build. I had to find a way to defuse it, and fast. So I decided to close my eyes, plug in my earphones, and *choose* to react with a FREEZE response instead, and to just come out of my surroundings and go into my own bubble.

We were stuck on the tarmac in Bulgaria for six hours, so I also had to really work on my patience, and accepting that I wasn't in control of the situation, and that blowing up wasn't going to help anyone – especially me.

But that doesn't mean I totally squashed my MOTIVATION to try to change and improve the situation, I just channeled it in a more productive way. When I got home, I wrote to the airline detailing Liam the Psycho Steward's behavior as calmly and factually as I could, and pointing out the amount of money he'd cost the airline as a result of his behavior.

Because I didn't come across like a ranting 'angry person' in the email, my complaint was taken much more seriously, and Liam was disciplined. Results!

PRACTICE LISTENING INSTEAD OF SPEAKING

MOTIVATORS are typically charismatic individuals with strong ideas and opinions that they aren't scared to express. While this is often a very useful skill, especially when we're trying to inspire and encourage others, it can also sometimes mean that MOTIVATORS end up eclipsing other people during conversations and discussions.

A quick hack to try to get our conversations more balanced is to make an active effort to practice *listening* as well as speaking. This could take the form of making a commitment to not interrupt other people when they're speaking until they've finished, even if we disagree with what they're saying or if we have something interesting we'd like to add.

ASK ABOUT OTHERS AND REALLY TAKE THE TIME TO LISTEN TO WHAT THEY TELL YOU

There's a difference between talking *to* people and talking *at* them, and this distinction is sometimes lost on MOTIVATORS. It can be a useful practice for MOTIVATORs to encourage other people to speak first, to ensure that the conversation is a two-way street, and doesn't turn into a monologue.

There's also a difference between *hearing* and *listening* that MOTIVATORS may need to work on developing. When we take the time to really *listen* to and internalize what the other person is saying, it affects us, and how we respond to them, in some obvious way. By contrast, when we're just hearing someone speak, it has no real impact on us or how we relate to them.

PUT YOURSELF IN OTHER PEOPLE'S SHOES

In the rush to impart our ideas, advice and insights, MOTIVATORS can sometimes ride a little roughshod over the feelings and opinions of others, and monopolize the discussion. Achieving true balance depends on developing a more flexible mindset that allows for differences of opinion and a different way of doing things.

We might not agree, we may have very strong views ourselves, and feel passionately about getting them across, but MOTIVATORS need to make a real effort to try to see where the other person is coming from and not just negate or dismiss other people's views. Often, just respecting the other person enough to hear them out can make all the difference in the world.

APOLOGIZE WHEN YOU HURT OTHER PEOPLE'S FEELINGS

MOTIVATORS can sometimes struggle with trying to project a 'perfect' persona to make it easier to get others to join them and accept what they're trying to say. However, we're all human beings, and occasionally, all of us will make mistakes.

Many MOTIVATORS have made the surprising discovery that showing some vulnerability and apologizing for mistakes and hurtful behavior not only doesn't damage their credibility and influence, but can actually boost it. Most people respond very positively to someone who's displaying the genuine humility required to apologize and own up to our flaws.

And apologizing also shows the other person that we're willing to police our own behavior, and to protect others from our lapses – which can be very important when dealing with powerful MOTIVATOR personalities who often have a pretty scary and intimidating side to them.

FRAME ADVICE AS 'TAKE IT OR LEAVE IT'

Don't try to force other people to accept your advice or to go along with your way of doing things even if it is the best in the world. An important part of getting more into balance as a MOTIVATOR is to respect other people's boundaries and freedom to choose to say 'no' – even if they're going to regret it later.

PRACTICE DELAYED GRATIFICATION

Many MOTIVATORS are goal-orientated and can find it very hard to put off achieving the goal or outcome they're after. In extreme cases, this can lead to them adopting strong-arm tactics to try and 'force' things through by the sheer dint of their personalities.

Sometimes that's an appropriate response – but not always. A good way for MOTIVATORS to build more resilience and patience is to practice delaying gratification on the small stuff that really doesn't matter so much. What I'm going to tell you sounds a little nuts, but it really works. Patience is built up incrementally. It's like a muscle that needs exercising.

Every time you put something off, you are giving your patience muscle a little work out.

And you can build it up quickly by getting into the habit of not giving yourself whatever you want, whenever you want it. You want to have some chocolate now? Wait a minute or two. You're itching to give someone a piece of your mind? Hold off for a minute, then speak. You want your kid to do the dishes, or walk the dog? Give them some space to decide when they can fit that into their schedule, and don't demand instant compliance.

The more you can practice delayed gratification in the areas that don't matter so much, the easier you'll find it to hold back a FIGHT response, and to choose the best way forward when it comes to things that really do matter.

BALANCED CONNECTION

Moving from Worry, Over-thinking and Running Away to Calm Acceptance of Feelings and Reality

CONNECTION'S MAIN STRESS RESPONSE IS: FLIGHT

With their quick thinking, innovation and industriousness, Connectors have the brain power to solve problems and create exciting new synergies between information, ideas, and most importantly of all, people.

They are really in their element in the world of ideas, and many Connectors excel at dissecting knowledge and communicating ideas to others. But the main difficulty for Connectors is that when they're stressed, they can get overwhelmed by their own thought processes and analytical capabilities, and / or by real or imagined fears, which can quickly spiral down into an anxious FLIGHT response away from reality and their own true feelings about things.

It's an irony, but while CONNECTORS excel at bringing ideas, information and people together externally, they often struggle to really connect to their own inner world, and particularly their emotions. But 'lost' emotions don't evaporate into thin air, they morph into other things. For CONNECTORS, their lost emotions usually transform into vague but powerful feelings of worry and anxiety.

Here are some of the main traits that CONNECTORS will need to focus on strengthening in order to achieve balance, and to start reconnecting to themselves:

- Acceptance
- Organization
- Tolerating discomfort without running away
- Developing the 'good enough' mindset

Let's go through these one by one.

ACCEPTANCE

When FLIGHT is jammed on, our heads start whirring with too many thoughts, our concentration goes out the window, and we might feel an overwhelming urge to literally run away.

But what are we really running from? The answer is all those undefined anxieties, worries and fears that are flitting around our brain and filling us full of panic.

Often, the biggest fear that's powering FLIGHT is the fear of doing something 'wrong'. If we do something wrong, then we might be blamed, or we might end up feeling bad, or we might have to deal with some big, raw emotions (ours and other people's….) and for a lot of CONNECTOR personalities, this sounds like a total disaster.

The fear of failure can keep the overachieving CONNECTOR in the office until midnight, obsessively trying to get all the details 'right'. Fear can be a great motivator in the short term, but over the medium to long-term, unless the CONNECTOR can figure out how to get a grip on the underlying fear that's fueling their FLIGHT stress response, they run the very real risk of breaking down or burning out.

The fear of things going wrong, and what that could lead to, is behind so much of the stress, running away and obsessive and compulsive behaviors that can dog an unbalanced CONNECTOR personality.

CHECK AND DOUBLE-CHECK

Michael is a highly intelligent polyglot who speaks seven languages fluently, and who also has a gift for mathematics. Unfortunately, due to a chaotic childhood that saw his parents divorcing when he was 11, and then long periods of time spent on different continents with different family members at different times, Michael never graduated from high school.

As an adult, he tried to remedy his lack of formal educational qualifications on a few different occasions, but he always ended up dropping out before he completed the requirements.

Michael suffers from extreme anxiety, with his thoughts whirring around his head a million times a second. He finds it very hard to relax, difficult to sleep through the night, and he spends most of his waking time worrying.

It's common for Michael to be half way up the street when he's suddenly assailed by doubts if he locked the front door or turned the gas off. When this occurs, he has to return to 'check and double-check', before he feels comfortable continuing his trip away from home. As a

CONNECTOR-MOTIVATOR, Michael can also veer off into angry rages when his anxiety overwhelms him, but his usual coping response is to run away.

Before the marriage of his daughter, Michael became so anxious about all the details that could possibly go wrong that he disappeared for two hours before the ceremony and no-one knew where he'd gone. Like many unbalanced CONNECTORS, Michael can be extremely good company socially, but has no real friends, always preferring to cut ties in anticipation of a relationship becoming too complicated and too much like hard work.

Michael refuses to accept that he is struggling with anxiety and worry, and he intensely dislikes talking about his 'feelings'. He gets angry when anyone tries to get him to open up about how he's really feeling, because Michael learned a long time ago that expressing his true feelings was unacceptable, and even dangerous.

As a grown up, his anger enables him to 'run away' from any discussion which might touch on the painful subject of his feelings, and it also enables him to stay disconnected from difficult feelings from his childhood. Perhaps, if Michael knew that the key to dissolving his anxiety lies in accepting and validating his feelings, he'd find the courage to open the lid of his inner Pandora's Box.

So, the main thing that CONNECTORS have to work on is accepting their own true feelings about things and airing out and addressing their unspoken fears.

The more we run away from our fears and worries, the bigger and more encompassing they seem to grow, and the more of a CONNECTOR'S energy and brain power they start to consume. The only way to start shrinking them down to a manageable size is to turn around and face them.

So a key lesson for CONNECTORS to learn is that problems and feelings don't just go away when we ignore them or try to hide from them – usually, they only intensify.

GET ORGANIZED

While footloose and fancy-free CONNECTORS often balk at the idea of getting a little more organized, unless they have a pronounced BUILDING side, introducing enough organization and structure to keep their inner uncertainty at manageable levels is a core skill that CONNECTORS need to learn.

That doesn't mean CONNECTORS can't perform effectively or efficiently, particularly at work, and especially if they are using their work as a way of escaping from their inner anxiety and fears. But often, the workaholic CONNECTOR is taxed to the limits of their mental endurance, and feeling permanently 'stressed out' makes them likely contenders for burn out, break down, or a heart-attack, God forbid.

What can help CONNECTORS keep a lid on obsessive thinking, worrying and overwhelm is simple things like regularly making lists, doing regular 'brain dumps', or mind-mapping. All these techniques can help CONNECTORS martial their thoughts, concretize their goals and responsibilities, and stop any slide into obsessive thinking or unspoken anxiety over the 'unknown'.

TOLERATE DISCOMFORT WITHOUT RUNNING AWAY

The main reason we run is because we feel threatened or endangered. When we've lost touch with what we truly feel, those lost emotions are often replaced by a vague feeling of anxiety and worry that can persuade us that something 'bad' is about to come out of the shadows at any moment.

As we mentioned above, CONNECTORS tend to be cerebral beings – they think things through, but they typically don't FEEL things. CONNECTORs often react to life's challenges rationally and thoughtfully, but rarely emotionally. And that's a shame, because our feelings can provide us with a very rich additional layer of information, knowledge and guidance, which are all highly-prized by CONNECTORS.

The hallmark of the unbalanced CONNECTORS is that they tend to always be rushing around DOING instead of taking some quiet time to BE, and to connect to their inner dimension. Unbalanced CONNECTORS typically avoid deep interactions with others, even their partners and spouses; because they feel very uncomfortable about the idea of exploring what they truly feel about their life, relationships and dreams. That's terrifying for a lot of people.

But as part of getting balanced, it's useful for CONNECTORS to adopt a more PHILOSOPHICAL THINKING frame of mind and to start asking themselves questions like, "Why am I pushing this off? What am I scared is going to happen? What am I really worrying about? What do I not want to face, either about myself or about my situation? What do I really *feel*?"

The more CONNECTORs can tolerate the discomfort of peeking into their own inner world, even if only for a little while, the less anxiety and worry they'll experience over time.

DEVELOP THE 'GOOD ENOUGH' MINDSET

CONNECTORS can be more prone to micro-managing and perfecting the details than any other personality group. But micro-managing is a very stressful habit to have! It's useful for CONNECTORS to practice stepping back a little and to work on accepting that things don't have to perfect, they just have to be good enough.

How we define 'good enough' in practice is something for each person to explore. But once we start pulling the idea of what constitutes 'good enough' into reality, it gets way easier to actually start to figure things through in a more realistic and grounded way.

Sure, we all want to have six pack abs and perfectly toned buttocks. But do we really feel like getting up at 5am every morning to run 10 miles come rain, sun or high water? What if we can't or won't do that, what's a 'good enough' option to staying fit in a less obsessive way that will still help us achieve our goals?

Detail-oriented CONNECTORS will benefit greatly from moving away from doing things perfectly to doing things to the standard of 'good enough', and will often find that they are able to achieve far more, with far less stress, once they make this mental shift.

CONNECTORS can counter their 'extreme inner perfectionist', who wants everything to be 100% perfect, 100% of the time, by taking the time to scope out 'good enough' outcomes, and by addressing the potential pitfalls and benefits that the 'good enough' approach offers versus 'perfection'.

Often, when the unreasonable expectation to do things 'perfectly' eases off, the CONNECTOR will be pleasantly surprised at how much their stress starts to reduce, how much more they start to enjoy the process they are engaged in, and how much better the outcome actually turns out to be.

MICRO-MANAGING ONLINE

Tim had a new business offering top-quality first-aid kits online, and he hired Emma to build him a website that would really stand out from the crowd. As a driven CONNECTOR-BUILDER, Tim had innovative ideas about how he wanted the site to look and function, but quickly ran into difficulties communicating his vision to Emma, a MOTIVATOR-PHILOSOPHER with her own strong ideas of how things should be done from a 'big picture' perspective.

The two started to clash as Tim increasingly drove Emma crazy with his requests that certain words and images should be moved 'two pixels' to the left, while Emma was still focused on trying to get the back-end of the site to function properly.

Every time Emma wanted a meeting to discuss the problems they were having on the site, Tim was too busy to attend. As the deadline loomed, Tim became even more focused on perfecting the tiny details, while Emma was becoming increasingly frustrated with Tim's micro-management and problem-avoidance. A week before the site was meant to launch, Emma quit.

Tim had to scramble to find another developer, so the site launched two months later than planned, causing Tim a lot of additional stress and anxiety. And even then, it still wasn't perfect.

QUICK WINS TO BALANCE CONNECTION

Try introducing one, some or even all of the following hacks, to get more into the 'balanced' mode.

LEARN HOW TO MIND-MAP

As mentioned above, mind-mapping is a great tool to enable CONNECTORS to 'dump' all of their thoughts onto a big piece of paper to make some space in their heads. Mind-maps can be used as one big, overgrown list, or can be done in a more sophisticated way as a problem-solving tool, or even a roadmap to the CONNECTORS often obscure inner world.

Whichever way you use mind-maps, they are very useful for 'unwinding' overwrought brains and thinking processes and helping CONNECTORS slow down their thinking.

FOCUS ON ONE THING AT A TIME

Multi-tasking comes very easily to CONNECTORS and can be a useful skill to have. But, multi-tasking can also be extremely stressful. When we have too many mental tabs open, when we have too many projects running at once, that takes up a lot of bandwidth and can really exacerbate underlying feelings of anxiety and worry.

It's not easy for CONNECTORS to slow down, but it's a crucial part of starting to defuse feelings of anxiety, panic and worry. Don't try and do too much at once, focus on one thing at a time and then move on.

A lot of our anxiety comes from uncertainty. Setting reasonable milestones and goals and focusing on one thing at a time is often a very effective way of closing down some of the mental windows and preventing feelings of panic and overwhelm.

MINIMIZE UNCERTAINTY

CONNECTORS can wake up in the morning with their hearts racing, thinking about the billions of important things they have to get done that day, and feeling increasingly panicked and stressed with every additional second. (Remember, panic and anxiety are classic manifestations of the FLIGHT stress response.)

A great antidote to this is to take a few minutes at the beginning of the day to really figure out what's required from the next 12 hours, and to set the priorities for the day ahead. Often, when we get to grips with what we really need to do and prioritize what we need to do, it turns out to be far less overwhelming, difficult or time-consuming than we actually think.

MINDFULNESS MEDITATION

Mindfulness meditation can mean many things to many people, and you could literally write a book – or ten – on this topic. But the two aspects of mindfulness meditation that are useful for CONNECTORS is making time for introspection, and learning how to breathe slowly and deeply.

When we feel anxious and panicked our breathing gets shallow. Taking a few deep breaths instantly sends a message to the body to calm down and stop stressing, and can stop a FLIGHT response in its tracks.

The other main benefit of regular mindfulness meditation is that it can gently get CONNECTORS used to 'being' instead of constantly doing, and can provide them with a safe space to start to identify and connect with some of their true feelings about things. Just notice your feelings, and start to explore what's really hiding out underneath any vague feelings of anxiety, worry or panic.

Mindfulness meditation can also help to 'ground' CONNECTORS into their feelings by forcing them to be present in the moment, pulling them into their bodies and out of their thoughts.

WALK OFF NERVOUS AGITATION

There's a strong 'body' component to the FLIGHT response. When we feel full of FLIGHT-induced mental agitation and nervous energy – we're pacing the room, jiggling our leg, swinging backwards and forward on the desk chair, or standing up then sitting down again, unable to settle down – one of the fastest and most effective ways to get the nervous energy to dissipate is to take a brisk walk, or do some other physical activity or exercise.

Once the FLIGHT energy has been moved out of our physical system, our minds will feel calmer and we'll find it easier to think again.

EAT FOR CALM

There are more and more scientific studies being done showing that anxiety and panic attacks are often connected to the brain not getting enough of the right nutrients. In one recent study in Japan, for example, researchers found that the subjects who had lower levels of B6 and Iron were far more prone to experiencing anxiety, panic attacks and hyperventilation.

The RESOURCES section has more ideas for getting educated on this topic, but it's important to make the link between good emotional health and getting enough of the right vitamins and minerals.

LIMIT YOUR ONLINE ACTIVITIES

This probably won't come as a newsflash (pardon the pun), but regularly checking news sites, emails and other social media feeds has been proven to increase feelings of stress, worry and anxiety.

While it's not so easy to deal with an internet addiction in our fast-paced, switched-on world, there are still a number of things you can do to try to limit your online activities and lower your stress. The RESOURCES section has more information on some practical things you can try to limit stress and anxiety-inducing habits online.

BALANCED PHILOSOPHICAL THINKING

Moving from apathy and unrealistic idealism to motivated action

PHILOSOPHICAL THINKING'S MAIN STRESS RESPONSE IS: FREEZE

With their strong idealistic streak and desire to know the truth, whatever the cost, the PHILOSOPHER personalities often act as the world's conscience. Their deep reflection, emotional sensitivity and awareness means they can dive beneath the surface to accurately assess situations and people.

PHILOSOPHERS are strongly connected to feelings – both their own and other people's – but as well as being their biggest gift, their strong emotional awareness can also provide them with their biggest challenge, especially when they get bogged down in unrealistic idealism and the despair and apathy that come along with the FREEZE stress response.

Life can get very heavy, very fast for PHILOSOPHERS, and they need to be on guard against disconnecting from the world when it all gets too much, or buying into the idea that nothing they do is going to make enough of a difference to make it worth the time and effort.

Here are some of the main traits that PHILSOPHERS will need to focus on strengthening in order to achieve balance and replace apathy, giving up, and feeling depressed with some of the self-motivation, optimism and energy that typically characterizes the MOTIVATORS and CONNECTORS.

- Taking responsibility
- Motivation
- Tenacity and trying again
- Setting goals
- Gratitude

Let's go through these one by one.

TAKING RESPONSIBILITY

PHILOSOPHERS are prone to FREEZE stress responses. Extreme FREEZEs are commonly referred to as clinical depressions, and sometimes they can last for months or even years.

As an unbalanced Motivator-Philosopher, I suffered from really severe depressions myself for the best part of three decades, and I know how hard it is to do anything, and just how heavy, disconnected and helpless we can feel when a FREEZE episode hits us full force.

So, when I talk about 'taking responsibility', I don't mean that you should just drag yourself out of bed, stop crying and go for a three hour jog to somehow snap yourself out of feeling depressed. I know from my personal experience that we just can't do that. The focus at this point is on *preventing* the depression from settling in on us when it's starting to descend.

What I'm talking about is coming to grips with the habits and thought-processes that effectively flip us into FREEZE, because when we start to recognize them at an earlier stage, we can stop them in their tracks.

The first priority for PHILOSOPHERS is to figure out the warning signs that a FREEZE episode is starting to manifest, so we can take actions to nip it in the bud at that point. For most people, these initial signs will be a brain fog and heaviness descending on us that makes us feel like we're physically sinking and becoming heavier and heavier, or 'freezing' in place.

As soon as those tell-tale signs begin, stand up and start to move. Dance, jog, go for a brisk walk, play soccer, throw a Frisbee around, something. Nine times out of ten, this is enough to stop a FREEZE state in its tracks.

The second priority for PHILOSOPHERS is to figure out who, or what, may have sparked that FREEZE reaction, because depressions and FREEZES don't come out of nowhere and drop on us like a thunderbolt. Start thinking about the people and situations that make you feel like you're worthless, totally unimportant and don't count for anything.

So often, that's what sparks the FREEZE state, and our job is to take the responsibility for figuring out who and what is triggering that state and how they are doing it, so we can take steps to prevent it from happening again in the future.

MOTIVATION

The next thing for PHILOSOPHERS to work towards is acquiring some motivation to improve their lot in life and to start chipping away or changing some of the situations that are making them miserable instead of giving up and going into hibernation.

MOTIVATION can come from one of three main places. Either, we can tap into some of the passion and determination of the MOTIVATORS, the fear of failure that's powering the CONNECTORS, or some of the desire to help others that comes from the BUILDERS.

If you've been stuck in apathy and non-movement for a while, then the fastest way to acquire some motivation and re-connect to the feeling that you are worth something is to come out fighting for yourself. I don't mean that you should go punch anyone in the face or have a sharp conversation or anything like that.

But coming out of a deep FREEZE state nearly always requires us to reattach to our feelings of anger, or FIGHT. Correctly identifying who and what we're angry at is often all we need to snap out of FREEZE, and to start acquiring the motivation we need to start looking after ourselves properly, and to interact with the outside world again.

TENACITY AND TRYING AGAIN

Unbalanced PHILOSOPHERS can easily get stuck in an apathetic, hibernation mode where everything – even really basic things like just brushing our teeth – just starts to feel like way too much effort.

In sharp comparison to MOTIVATORS and CONNECTORS who tend to speed up under stress, PHILOSOPHERS tend to slow down, and even come to a complete halt, especially when faced with challenges and difficulties.

While we don't want the unbalanced CONNECTOR's anxiety-fueled perfectionism and overworking, or the unbalanced MOTIVATOR's angry bull-dozer approach to life, we do want a bit of their energy.

What can help PHILOSOPHERS greatly is to work on strengthening their determination and tenacity. Deep-thinking and reflective PHILOSOPHERs often have a lot of natural inertia, and that can easily translate into a tendency to give up at the first hurdle and go back into hibernation.

Counter this by making a promise to yourself that whatever commitment you make, you are going to *stick to it*, come what may. Start small and look for quick wins, initially, that will help you build a momentum and keep you moving forward. A little tenacity can go a long, long way in helping PHILOSOPHERS achieve more balance.

SET GOALS

An important part of staying accountable to yourself is setting goals. PHILOSOPHER personalities can often lose their motivation by setting unrealistic or idealistic goals that bear very little relation to reality, are too pie in the sky, or simply way too ambitious. Setting regular goals and working towards specific aims and milestones can help PHILOSOPHERS inject some much-needed movement and direction into their plans.

It's a good idea to keep the goals reasonable, and to start very small, especially at the beginning. Go step by step, and check in with your progress every single day to see where you're really holding.

Over time, as PHILOSOPHERS start to pull out of the FREEZE stress response, they often find that their dreams for the future start to get a little bigger, their confidence in sharing their wisdom with the outside world starts to grow, and that they start to get way more motivated to engage with others and to make some real change in the world.

GRATITUDE

Under stress, PHILOSOPHER personalities often struggle with feelings that the world is pointless, that life is 'flat' and empty, and that there is nothing good about themselves or their life. Working on feeling gratitude can be another powerful way of breaking the grip of these FREEZE-induced notions.

Ultimately, FREEZE boils down to self-abandonment and 'playing dead'. It's like we don't care about anything or anyone. But really? That's not true. If we couldn't get a cup of coffee, or a comfortable pair of shoes, or if our shower was broken or we couldn't pay the rent, that would still upset us greatly.

So, what the habit of gratitude does is encourage us to flip on its head how we relate to all these things we often take for granted. Gratitude is really just making a regular habit of noticing all the good things – and people, and opportunities, and experiences - that we have in in our life that we would miss greatly if they weren't there.

Making the effort to count our blessing in this way reinforces the understanding that we actually have a lot to lose – and still a lot to fight for. Practicing gratitude helps us appreciate that our life is valuable, and that our ideas and idealism are worth fighting for.

While the FIGHT response certainly has its drawbacks, it's still one of the best – and instantaneous – motivators and energizers, and a very powerful way to pull out of a potential FREEZE nose-dive.

MOVING OUT OF RANGE

Rupert hated bringing his girlfriends home to meet his family, mostly because of his older brother, Ed. Ed and Rupert had never gotten along that well as kids, but as adults, they could barely stand each other. Rupert was a more introverted Philosopher-Builder, while Ed was a flamboyant Motivator-Connector, who had a flair for turning heads and always having the last word.

Rupert felt invisible around Ed, and hated the obvious interest his charismatic brother elicited from his dates. Rupert usually reacted to Ed's stealing the show by shrinking into his shell and turning sullen. Unwilling to make a scene publically, he'd given up trying to compete with Ed a long time ago, and now he just resigned himself to feeling like an invisible loser, stuck in his brother's shadow.

Usually, Rupert would go and sit somewhere quiet and start watching *Game of Thrones,* sullenly waiting for his girlfriend to even notice that he was gone. Sometimes he could watch a whole episode…

Until one day Rupert realized that going into a deep FREEZE wasn't helping to improve the situation and that something needed to change. Following the principle of attaining Inner Balance to achieve Outer Balance in relationships, Rupert realized that he needed to approach the problem in a radically different way.

In place of giving up and spacing out in front of the screen, he either needed some 'angry' motivation to confront his brother, or some of the Connectors' ability to keep changing things up and trying new ways of handling the problem instead of sullenly accepting it.

Rupert thought an angry confrontation with Ed would probably only backfire, so instead, he used his PHILOSOPHICAL THINKING to really drill down, to uncover the core of the problem. Rupert realized that continuing to live at home was 'comfortable' in a lot of ways, but was keeping him stuck in an immature frame of mind, with Ed as the cherry on top of the problem.

With this new understanding, Rupert was able to tap into some MOTIVATION to start making plans to move out.

QUIK WINS TO BALANCE PHILOSOPHICAL THINKING

Try introducing one, some or even all of the following hacks to get more into the 'balanced' mode:

GET ENOUGH EXERCISE

While all personality types can benefit from regular exercise, it's particularly important for PHILOSOPHER personalities to ensure that they are breaking a sweat for a bare minimum of 20 minutes, at least three times a week.

FREEZE stress reactions can quickly spiral into a depression, and regular exercise is one of the very best natural ways of overcoming that sense of heaviness and inertia, which are the body's warning signals that it's starting to shut down.

If you feel the heaviness and brain-fog descending – get off the couch, stop staring into space, and make yourself do something active. Dance, go for a brisk walk around the block, grab a rag and starting cleaning the windows – it doesn't matter *what*, as long as you keep moving until the sense of heaviness dissipates.

MAKE A NEW START

It's very easy for PHILOSOPHERS to get stuck in the past, reliving experiences and situations in their head that may well be limiting their ability to change or try something new in the present.

Here's where it's good to borrow some of the CONNECTORS' ability to swiftly disconnect and try something new. New starts typically come packaged with a lot of motivation, energy and excitement about what's to come – which is exactly what a lot of PHILOSOPHERS need to counter the "I can't be bothered" tendency.

It can be something as simple as trying a different recipe for supper, taking a different route to work, or buying a piece of clothing in a totally different color. Making a new start is also the secret to standing back up again after life knocks us down.

DON'T TAKE THINGS SO MUCH TO HEART

Idealistic, emotional PHILOSOPHERS can often go into hibernation mode as a form of 'protest' at the world. Sometimes, it's easier to disappear into a mental bubble than to interact in a society that is filled with so much darkness and cruelty.

But if the 'conscience' of the world goes AWOL, who's going to be left to make things change? PHILOSOPHERS have to learn how to keep the world's problems at arms' length a little so they don't get totally overwhelmed and then taken out by them.

Yes, starving kids is bad, yes, rising tides of plastic bottles is terrible – but taking all this stuff to heart and then falling into a depression about it isn't going to help anyone. The 'reality' of bad situations needs to be tempered with joyful experiences, practical attempts to change things up, and (whisper it…) *fun*.

Unlike the other personalities, PHILOSOPHERS generally have no problem facing the truth, honestly exploring difficult issues, or acknowledging their own negative feelings about things. But it's hard to walk around with the weight of the world 24/7 without getting pulled into sadness and depression.

So lighten things up, take regular breaks from the heavy stuff, and also make sure you're doing things that just make you plain old happy. (Yes, eating chocolate is definitely on that list.)

STOP WAITING FOR PRINCE CHARMING TO SHOW UP

Of all the many, many sins to be laid at Disney's door, telling us fairy stories where 'Prince Charming' shows up to rescue the damsel in distress is towards the top of the pile.

With their vivid imaginations and pull to idealistic outcomes, PHILOSOPHERS can waste half their life waiting for some external 'Prince Charming' to come and rescue them from their problems, and then feel bitterly disappointed and let down when that doesn't happen.

But once the PHILOSOPHER internalizes that they have to take responsibility for themselves – which means finding a way to change whatever they can't accept, and accepting the reality of whatever they can't change – that's when the inertia starts to evaporate and things can really start to move.

MINIMIZE SCREEN TIME

While CONNECTORS can get lost in gathering information and checking emails, PHILOSOPHERS can get totally swept up in fantasies and alternative universes where they can lose themselves by living life vicariously through the screen.

Trouble is, once you've finished binge-playing World of War, or Sim Nation, or finished watching a whole season of Stranger Things back-to-back on Netflix – real life is still waiting for you with its dirty dishes, bills to pay, and all the other complications you were trying to escape from.

So now you're going to feel even worse than you did before you ran away into the screen. Spending too much time online isn't a great idea for anyone, but with their innate pull to inertia and getting lost in their imaginations, it can be particularly harmful and addictive for PHILOSOPHERS.

There are a number of different tools out there that can help you minimize your screen time and come to grips with an internet addiction. You can find some to get you started in the RESOURCES section at the back of the book.

BALANCED BUILDING

Moving from superficial interactions and passive aggression to authentic and truthful self-expression

BUILDING'S MAIN STRESS RESPONSE IS: FREEZE

BUILDERS are the salt-of-the-earth people who often function as the 'glue' that holds society together. With their practical, no-nonsense approach to life, craving for stability and willingness to accept others 'as is', BUILDERS can make a loyal friend or worker for life.

Where MOTIVATORS inspire, CONNECTORS think and PHILOSOPHERS feel, BUILDERS just get on and do. However, the downside of being so accepting and preferring 'the devil you know' is that BUILDERS can end up living life in a very superficial way, where comfort becomes the main goal to strive for and the priority to maintain at all costs.

When under stress, BUILDERS usually react by going into FLATTER mode. The main challenges for people stuck in FLATTER mode tend to come as the 'absences' of positive things, like being able to express themselves truthfully, and being able to get past the 'polite' stage in relationships and interactions into being able to really communicate on a deep soul level.

Society hasn't really figured out the true cost of the FLATTER stress response yet, but it's underlying all the political correctness that's squeezing the joy, vitality and sincerity out of human interactions, and leaving us feeling deeply lonely. Flattering evil behavior instead of finding it and confronting it can also be a problem for BUILDERS who unwittingly then enable it to continue.

With their innately kind and helpful natures, and difficulty in asserting themselves and putting themselves first, BUILDERS are the most prone to being exploited and mistreated by others.

If FLATTER is your main stress response, then the main work to do to get into balance will revolve around the following things:

- Putting yourself first
- Truthful self-expression
- Appropriate boundaries
- Authenticity
- Assertion

Let's go through each one.

PUTTING YOURSELF FIRST

BUILDERS are often far more consciously attuned to other people's feelings and moods than to their own. Where MOTIVATORS can become over-focused on **me first**, BUILDERS can totally lose their sense of self in the process of trying to keep everyone else happy.

As a result, BUILDERS often feel blank and confused when asked what they really think or feel about something, and they can literally lack the vocabulary required to attach a feeling to the word that describes it.

So a key balancing trait for BUILDERS to work on is to re-discover their sense of self, and to explore what their own preferences are, what their own opinions are, and what they truly think and feel about things, so that at least occasionally they can start to put themselves first.

TRUTHFUL SELF-EXPRESSION

Another balancing trait for BUILDERS to prioritize is working on expressing themselves more truthfully to others. That doesn't necessarily mean to go out and tell everyone exactly what we think. Rather, it's more the process of expressing ourselves more truthfully, particularly *to ourselves*.

Superficiality blossoms when people are expected to swallow their true feelings, their true thoughts, and to not rock the boat. Allowing ourselves to acknowledge what we really think and feel about things is liberating, but also potentially scary. Giving a voice to our truthful self-expression could lead to some big changes in our life, relationships and priorities, which is often why so many peace-loving BUILDERS shy away from it.

SETTING APPROPRIATE BOUNDARIES

Many unbalanced BUILDERS can end up living much of their lives according to the dictates and desires of other people. Especially at the beginning of the 'getting balanced' process, it's going to be important to put appropriate boundaries in place while we are growing our ability to think and choose for ourselves.

Visualizations and role playing can greatly help here, where we actually think through a situation or encounter before or after it happens, and imagine how we would like it to be, or what we would like to do differently next time around.

Just setting the intention will get our minds engaged in making it happen, and start to change the way we usually handle potential confrontations and difficult conversations.

STRIVE FOR AUTHENTICITY

Sometimes we have to keep our mouths shut, and we have to play the game and keep up appearances. That's the world we live in. But it's important for BUILDERS to work on not getting totally lost in the pretense, and to work on truly being themselves – even if that's not always so popular with others.

When people get stuck in a long-term FLATTER response where their relationships are built on putting themselves out for others, they often have an extremely hard time honestly asking for the things they would like or need, or expecting healthy reciprocation.

Once BUILDERS start to connect more to their own emotions and thoughts, the process of becoming more authentic will start to move.

A word of caution here, though. At the beginning of getting more balanced from a polarized FLATTER response, many BUILDERS can experience a scary lurch into FIGHT territory where they suddenly discover they have a temper, and can feel angry and upset. Don't panic if this happens! Just as PHILOSOPHERS often need some of the FIGHT / FLIGHT energy to snap them out of their 'passive' state, the same is true for BUILDERS.

Unbalanced BUILDERS often also need some of the motivation and determination associated with FIGHT to start asserting themselves in a healthier, more authentic way, and some of the movement and renewal of FLIGHT to propel them out of their superficial and suffocating comfort zone.

Easy does it, but getting in touch with their true emotions can give BUILDERS access to the range of human experience they may be currently missing out on. That's not always or uniformly 'positive' or 'happy', but it's emotionally healthy, and will open up all sorts of new paths and opportunities to enable authentic self-expression and genuinely fulfilling relationships.

QUICK WINS TO BALANCE BUILDING

Try introducing one, some, or even all of the following hacks to get more into the 'balanced' mode:

PRACTICE SAYING 'NO'

Start small, but start practicing saying 'no' without feeling guilty or bad. It's often easier to start doing this with complete strangers than it is close to home, and we're not talking about ripping people's head off, here. Simply start exercising the muscle we all have called 'free choice', and get into the habit of only saying 'yes' – to favors, ideas, suggestions and requests – if that's what you really want to do.

CHECK IN WITH YOUR BODY

While all unbalanced personality types can suffer from somatic illness and pain, the problem can be particularly acute for BUILDER types. Start to pay attention to your body to see what clues and messages it's telling you about how you really may be feeling about certain people or situations.

Do they energize, or drain you? Are you getting strange stomachaches or headaches when you interact with certain people, or engage in certain behaviors? Does your voice suddenly disappear in the middle of a conversation, or does your back start to twinge?

All of these can be subtle, but potent clues from your body to you that you're actually not as comfortable or happy in a particular situation or exchange as you may think.

CREATE A LIST OF PRIORITIES

BUILDERS can often find themselves in difficulties because they overpromise and run themselves ragged trying to do too many favors for too many people. As part of the process of getting to know what your own preferences and feelings are, put some time aside to create a list of priorities.

List the people in your life, and prioritize who you want to spend more of your time with, and whose requests should get top billing. You can also prioritize which causes are closest to your heart, and also what types of activities and 'favors' you most enjoy.

Increasingly, look to spend more of your time doing the things towards the top of your list, for the people you most care about.

PRACTICE MAKING DECISIONS

Again, start small! You don't have to dive in the deep end here and make big decisions about relocating to a different country (unless you really want to…) The idea is to start to feel out what you prefer, and what you really think in a myriad small ways, instead of deferring to others.

GREG'S TABLE DÉCOR

Greg grew up in a home where his overbearing Motivator-Builder mother made all the decisions and called all the shots from what Matt should eat for supper to what style of clothes he should buy.

After Greg, a Pure Builder, got married, his wife Angie found herself stepping into her mother-in-law's shoes. Greg was pleasant and helpful, but totally passive in the relationship and hardly ever took the initiative on anything from deciding where they should go on holiday to picking a color to paint the spare bedroom.

Angie, a Philosopher-Motivator, found herself making too many of the decisions about too many aspects of their life together, which initially her MOTIVATOR side quite liked. But as the years passed, Angie's PHILOSOPHER started to ring the alarm bells that something wasn't quite right with Greg's 'absent' and unengaged approach to life.

Increasingly, Angie started to feel like she was living with Mr. Invisible, a lodger who paid his share of the mortgage and did whatever the landlady (i.e. Angie) told him to do, but who was otherwise 'missing'. Even when Angie asked him a simple question like what he wanted to eat for supper, Greg came up blank.

After talking about the problem with her therapist, Angie realized that Greg was petrified of being attacked for somehow making the wrong decision or 'rocking the boat', even on the most mundane issues. The therapist suggested that Angie create a 'safe space' where Greg could start to practice decision-making where there were no real consequences for making the wrong choice.

Angie came home and told Greg he was now responsible for making the dinner table look nice. He could do it whichever way he wanted – with flowers or without, formal dinnerware or paper plates, any type of napkins he wanted, place names, etc., but it was totally his call. Greg thought the idea was ridiculous to start with, but was happy to do it to keep his wife happy.

It took a few months of picking paper napkins before Greg realized that he was starting to develop some real preferences for how the table should look. Greg's growing self-awareness spread out into more and more areas of his life until a couple of years after the table décor experiment began Greg quit his office job, with Angie's support, to open his own homeware store.

TRY BLUE SKY THINKING

If you could have anything in life, what would you pick? Take a big piece of paper and spend a bit of time writing down what car you'd drive, what job you'd do, where you'd vacation, who your perfect partner would be, what sort of house you'd live in and who you'd hang out with.

Don't overthink and don't self-censor. The idea is to just get in touch with your own preferences and dreams, however unrealistic or far-fetched they might be, and to give yourself permission to express your own thoughts and ideas.

STEP OUT OF THE COMFORT ZONE

BUILDERS typically like stability and predictability, but stepping out of the comfort zone is a vital component of becoming more balanced. Change up the brand of coffee you drink, or the ketchup you buy, take a different route to work, watch a film on a subject you know nothing about, or read a website that's on the opposite side of the spectrum from the sites you usually go to for information.

Every time you challenge yourself to adapt to a slightly new or different way of doing things, you're expanding your tolerance for change, and ensuring that 'stable' doesn't degenerate into boring and stagnant.

LIMIT SOCIAL MEDIA

Unbalanced BUILDERS are often strongly attracted to social media where appearance is all there really is and relationships never progress past the 'like' stage. But spending time on social media tends to only reinforce the BUILDING tendency towards superficiality, passive reaction and 'group think' instead of independent analysis, active communication and deep discussion.

NEXT STEPS

We've covered an awful lot of ground over the last few chapters, so I just want to round things off by summing up the main points of the PEOPLE SMARTS SYSTEM before leaving you with some suggestions on how you can take this further, if you want to.

All of us are a mix of the four building blocks of personality, MOTIVATION, CONNECTION, PHILOSOPHICAL THINKING and BUILDING. When we get stressed, the negative side of our personality tends to come to the fore, and will manifest itself as either a FIGHT, FLIGHT, FREEZE or FLATTER response, depending on what our personality type is.

While modern science tends to focus on the negative aspects of our personalities and to put across the message that we're basically stuck with our negative traits and extreme reactions to stress, the PEOPLE SMARTS SYSTEM takes a very different view of people and their personality traits.

PEOPLE SMARTS is based on that idea that in order for us to really tap into our unique potential as human beings, we just need to learn how to *balance* our particular mix of these four emotional states so that the positive side of our personalities come to the fore and the 'stressed-out', negative side starts to diminish.

The human psyche contains tremendous positive power, and PEOPLE SMARTS is all about accessing it and starting to channel all that energy in a more positive and helpful direction.

But before we can really do that, we need to understand that our personalities are built up from a unique mix of these four main states, and that there is no 'one size fits all' approach to good mental health.

Rather, we have to learn how to identify and play to our strengths, and also, how to identify and work on our weaknesses, to move to a place where we can access way more of the positive potential inside, without getting side-tracked and waylaid too much by our negative stress response.

Like I said way back at the beginning, even just reading this book will already give you a lot of insight into why you're reacting and acting the way you are, and how you can start to move from unbalanced, unhappy and stressed-out to emotionally healthy, happy and fulfilled.

If you'd like to take this further, I've developed a number of different resources on my website that can help you. As well as the PEOPLE SMARTS SYSTEM 16 Personalities online quiz, you can also find different interactive programs and courses that can help you start applying the PEOPLE SMARTS wisdom to your life and relationships.

All of us have a unique job to do in the world, as **ourselves**.

We don't need to try to be like anyone else, we just need to work with the raw material we were blessed with, reduce our subconscious overreactions to stress, and then let the **real us** get on with the job of building the world, and developing healthy and happy relationships the way it was always intended.

THE LAST WORD ON CRUSHING YOUR STRESS

I've packed a ton of useful information into this book, and I've also given you a thorough introduction to what the People Smarts stress personality system actually is, but if you want some additional help on crushing your stress, you might want to join me for the **Crush Your Stress Masterclass.**

The **Crush Your Stress Masterclass** is a 5 week online program specifically designed for people who regularly get angry, switch off, or run away when they're stressed, or who are finding that their over-reactions to stress are hurting their relationships and causing them problems.

If you're interested in joining me for the **Crush Your Stress Masterclass** you can pick between a self-guided course, or joining me for the live group coaching option. Either way, your mission, should you choose to accept it is to learn how to control your destructive reactions to stress in 5 weeks, so you can keep calm under pressure, stay present, stop overwhelm in its tracks, but still stand up for yourself, when you need to.

If that sounds interesting, you can learn more about the course and sign up for it here: **www.peoplesmartsacademy.com**

RESOURCES

Self-education is a very important part of the 'de-stressing' process. Simply learning about what might be causing you to act and react in a particular way is often enough to start to defuse an unhelpful stress response all by itself. I highly recommend the following books:

Connection: Emotional and Spiritual Growth Through Experiencing God'
    Presence – Efim Svirsky.

Complex PTSD - From Surviving to Thriving – Pete Walker.

Does Stress Damage the Brain? Understanding trauma-related disorders
    from a mind-body perspective. – J. Douglas Bremner.

It Didn't Start With You – Mark Wolynn.

Mindsight: The new science of personal transformation – Daniel J. Siegel

Running on Empty: Overcome Your Childhood Emotional Neglect –
    Jonice Webb.

The Body Keeps the Score: Brain, mind and body in the healing of trauma - Bessel Van Der Kolk.

The Body Remembers: The psychophysiology of trauma and trauma treatment (Volumes I and II) – Babette Rothschild.

The Promise of Energy Psychology: Revolutionary tools for dramatic personal change – David Feinstein, Donna Eden and Gary Craig.

The Revolutionary Trauma Release Process – David Bercelli.